THE ROAD FROM
MONEY

Enjoy

Sylvester Boyd J.

THE ROAD FROM
MONEY

A JOURNEY TO FIND WHY?

PART 1

(1925 - 1937)

SYLVESTER BOYD JR.

AuthorReputationPress®
Creativity & Branding

Author Reputation Press LLC
45 Dan Road Suite 5
Canton MA 02021
www.authorreputationpress.com
Hotline: 1(800) 220-7660
Fax: 1(855) 752-6001

Ordering Information:
Quantity sales. Special discounts are available on quantity purchases by corporations, associations, and others. For details, contact the publisher at the address above.

Printed in the United States of America.

ISBN-13:	Softcover	978-1-64961-257-1
	eBook	978-1-64961-258-8

Library of Congress Control Number: 2021904723

CONTENTS

DEDICATION

This book is dedicated to the men and women whose names are unknown.

My ancestors that were taken from their homeland, and placed in the belly of slave ships.

My ancestors that were subjected to unimaginable living conditions, aboard slave ships, and suffered brutality at the hands of slave traders.

My ancestors that were sold, and became the property of other human beings at slave auctions.

My ancestors that worked from sun up to sun down, picking and chopping cotton, cutting sugarcane and tobacco; cooking, building, and anything else the slave master ordered. This was all done for free, making the slave masters wealthy.

My ancestors that were not allowed to learn how to read, or write, and were given a new language.

My ancestors that were freed, but had no money, land or homes; only themselves after slavery. Only the strong survived this ordeal.

These were my ancestors that made my life possible in this country.

These are the shoulders that African-Americans stand on today. They should never be forgotten

ACKNOWLEDGMENTS

My deepest gratitude goes to my aunt, Estella Clemens, who inspired me to write this first novel. It is the first of a four-part series, built around her life's story. Also, to my great Grandfather, Paul Reynolds, whose wisdom has been passed down through the years. Thanks to my grandmother, Julia Irene Reynolds, who told me about the many family events that are revealed in this novel. Many thanks to my mother, Elizabeth James, who raised me and instilled in me the qualities of perseverance, respect for myself and others. And, to my Uncle Leroy Whitfield, who was a very important part of my life.

All the people mentioned gave me the insight to write this novel about life in America's deep South at the beginning of the 20th century. A very special thanks to my wife, Paulette Boyd, who helped me bring this novel into being and who gave the novel its title. In addition, my gratitude to Whitney Napoleon for her skills in art and design. Finally, to my publisher. Author Reputation Press, LLC, for their assistance.

CHAPTER 1

Why?

It was 1925, on a very warm spring day in Money, Mississippi. The sound of a steam locomotive puffing its way down the tracks pierced the calm that lay like a blanket over the small town. The locomotive left a tail of white, gray, and black smoke behind that mixed with the mist from the nearby Tallahatchie River. Two rabbits scurried across the tracks just before the slow-moving train. Beside the track an old mule-drawn wooden wagon moved slowly. Inside, eight-year-old Estella and her Grandfather, Paul Reynolds, a share-cropper, were making their way into town.

Today was a very special day for Estella—or Sister, as her family sometimes called her. It was her eighth birthday and she was going to spend it with her Grandfather. She was a smart, good-looking dark girl, just over four feet tall, with large eyes, and hair tied up in two pigtails. Today, she was barefoot, wanting to save her shoes for church services on Sunday. She was dressed in faded overalls, and always smiling and happy when she was with her loving Grandfather. Her father had left Money a year before—she wasn't sure why; but when she was with her Grandfather the world was perfect, and she got her way most of the time.

Arriving in town, Paul stopped the wagon in front of Benson's General Store and stepped down from the wagon seat. He was a dark-skinned, good-looking man, who had a bright smile and stood five feet, ten inches. Today he wore bib overalls and a white cotton shirt. He was always a smart dresser, with his ever-present pocket watch that had a long chain, which he kept with him always.

Estella looked down at her Grandfather as he lifted her from the wagon. He took her by the hand, and headed for the general store. Before they could cross the road, a wagon filled with cotton rumbled down the road toward them. On the back of the wagon sat Estella's big brother, Leroy, age eleven, who was working today loading in the fields and unloading cotton at the cotton gin. Leroy waved to his sister and Grandfather as he passed. He soon disappeared into a cloud of dust, on his way to the cotton gin.

Benson's General Store was the only store in the town. Like most of the buildings in town, it was wooden, with a small landing and steps leading up to an entrance. Its door had a big glass window in the center, with two smaller windows on each side of the door. Stepping inside, Estella and her Grandfather looked around to see who was there today. In this sleepy southern town, Paul was always observant about his environment, checking out the store. As a Negro—and a Negro man, too—Paul knew he had to be careful. Entering the store, they saw two middle-aged white men sitting near a big black pot-bellied stove in the center of the store. Mr. Benson, the owner, was behind the counter wearing a white apron. A round-faced white man was sitting by the stove wearing faded overalls, and talking to another white man, much younger than him. "When my baby brother bit by dat big rattlesnake, I didn't waste no time; and took out my pocket knife 'n cut open his leg where da snake bit. I sucked out da poison 'n spit it out."

"He live," asked his friend, a long-faced man with a reddish beard.

"Sho, he live! I got all da poison out; but he was sick for weeks." Walking toward the counter, Paul was about to ask Mr. Benson for the few items he needed. Suddenly a plump white woman with a pock-marked face entered the store and rushed over to the counter, stepping in front of Estella and Paul. Mr. Benson immediately turned to wait on the woman before them.

"We were here first." Estella told the woman.

"Niggers ain't never first," the woman snarled back. Estella was angry and bewildered, as she looked at Mr. Benson.

Mr. Benson snapped, "Gal, she just telling ya right!"

"Some people don't know right from wrong," her Grandfather replied.

"Watch yo' mouth, boy!" Mr. Benson scolded. "Ya bedda teach that gal da way things are in Money. If 'n ya don't, ya gonna get her in trouble. What ya niggers want, anyway?"

Estella still did not understand why the white woman should be able to step before them in line. Just then, an old white man entered the store, and again Mr. Benson waited on him first. After twenty minutes, Paul purchased some flour; one of the few food items sharecroppers bought from the general store—like salt, sugar, cornmeal, and pepper. They grew other fruits and vegetables to eat on their small plot and prepared it themselves. Because it was his granddaughter's birthday, Paul bought a birthday lollipop for her and together they left the store.

Outside Benson's Store, a young white man was coming down the walkway and darted before them. Paul quickly stepped aside giving him plenty of room to continue. Estella stepped aside, too, but she asked, "Why? Why we have to step aside fo' dem always? Why, Papa, why? And why Mr. Benson wait on white folks befo' us?"

"Estella, dis da way of Money 'n da South. But everyone knows it ain't right."

The young girl was still miffed as they climbed back in the old wagon. Paul shook the reins, but the mule did not move. He shook his reins again, but the stubborn brown-and-gray mule just stood there.

Estella had a serious look on her face. "Why some folks got horse-drawn carriages, and other folks got mule-drawn wagons, Papa?"

"Cause'n some folks, like some white folks, got money and can buy horses. Negro folks lucky to have a mule."

"But Papa, why dey got mo' money?"

"Cause'n they own the fields. Negro folks get nothin' but picking cotton, if dey lucky. Most of us sharecroppers pickin' cotton, gettin' paid next to nothin'."

"Somethin' ain't right—just ain't right, Papa."

"A lot ain't right. But I got somethin' fo' this lazy mule that don't wanna go." Paul reached in the back of the wagon, and grabbed an ingenious device he had made. It was a can with both sides cut out, and a bamboo cane pole running through it. He hooked the end of the pole over a nail to hold it in place. Paul grabbed a carrot from the back of the wagon, attached it to the other end of the pole, and extended the carrot before the mule. Seeing the carrot, the mule moved, trotting slowly down the road, past the cotton fields being worked by disheveled sharecroppers. Estella sucked on her

4

lollipop; her Grandfather could tell she was still upset over the scene at Benson's Store.

"Don't be scowlin' so, gal. Things like what happen in da store just now, with white folks wanna be served first, and havin' to step aside fo' white folks, 'cause bad things happen if ya don't step aside fo' dem, that's called hate. It's better now than befo' when my Mama and Pa was slaves. Now we can come and go as we please, and no one owns us. Back den, white folks told us when ya go to bed, when ta get up, what ta eat. If ya didn't do what dey say, ya got whipped or sold to a worse plantation. And ya couldn't keep up with yo family 'cause they got sold off to some other plantation."

"But it ain't right, Papa—they always treat'n us bad."

"Dis be da way it tis right now. It was worse for my folks back then. They was sold to a plantation over in Granada County. Mama told me that Pa was beat with a whip and that some slaves was taken by their master in the night. Some were never seen again. Maybe there will be a better day. Things just gotta get better fo' Negro folks. Ya need to get as much schoolin' as ya kin get, 'cause schoolin' move you ahead, gal." Paul shook the carrot and the mule moved a little faster, making its way along the road.

CHAPTER 2

The Cotton Fields

This was Estella's first year working in the cotton fields; she was eight, working with dozens of Negro adults and children her age and older. It was a hot fall day, with plenty of mosquitoes in the cotton field, but no one complained. In the spring and summer, she helped chop and pull weeds away from the cotton plants. Today, Estella carried heavy buckets of water for everyone to drink. Then she started picking cotton, grabbing the cotton buds quickly, trying to avoid the thorns that often pierced her fingers and under her fingernails. She tossed the buds in the pick sack she had suspended across her shoulder, which she dragged between cotton rows, filling it with as many cotton blossoms as possible.

Estella's six younger cousins were also working the cotton field, along with her Aunts. Her brother Leroy worked hard loading cotton on wagons—a man's job, and heavy work for a boy. Estella had a big rag, wiping the sweat from her face and neck, and ignored the mud on her feet and between her toes. She worked as fast as she could to fill the big bag with cotton so she could earn two cents today. She was saving her money, hiding it in a pouch she had in her pocket. She had no idea why, or what she would buy with the money one day, but she knew money was important. The way white folks always tried to keep Negro people poor made that evident. At her young age, she knew that when you have the chance to earn money, it is best that you hold on to as much of it as you can.

Halfway through the day, wiping sweat from her brow, she went to the wagon where Leroy was loading cotton, telling him, "I can do dat, quicker than ya…."

"Get on away from here, gal; you always be thinkin' ya better than me!"

His sister just laughed, and went back to picking cotton, filling her long heavy bag. Just before the end of the work day, a loud scream was heard in the fields. The screams continued even louder; Estella and the other workers began to run toward the screams, through the rows of cotton plants. They found Ruth Jessup, a girl just fourteen years old, lying on the ground—as a rattlesnake slithered away between the cotton plants.

"A rattlesnake done bit her," Estella's Aunt Mattie cried out.

Ruth was in pain, still screaming, as she held her leg. They all looked at Ruth bewildered.

Estella asked, "Any of ya got a knife?"

"I got one," replied her brother, as he pulled out a knife he used to cut cotton bale strings.

Estella took the knife and kneeled on the ground beside Ruth. She wiped the knife with her rag and slit the bleeding snake bite, remembering what she overheard from the man in Benson's Store. She sucked the poison from the bite and spit it out.

Everyone looked on amazed, as Ruth held her leg, moaning. Paul came running with a pail of water, and Estella rinsed her mouth a dozen times to clear it of the poison.

"Where ya learn dat, gal?" asked her Aunt.

"I think dat gal know everything," said Leroy.

"I overheard it from two white men in Benson's Store. It's hot and late; let's get to dat river."

Just then the work bell rang—it was quitting time. Everyone dragged their bags nearly overflowing with cotton to a big wagon. An old red-haired white man weighed each bag—Estella smiled when he gave her two cents.

As the grown-ups headed from the field, all the children burst out running down the narrow road. They passed people walking, and several wagons going by, as a light mist covered the nearby fields. Estella, Leroy, and their six cousins were running fast, seeing who ran the fastest. Suddenly they stopped. Everyone stepped to the side of road, surprised to see a Model T automobile in the distance coming toward them. As the automobile neared, they saw a well-dressed white couple inside smiling proudly, for owning the advanced machine. The automobile kicked up plenty of dust on the road and the driver wore goggles to keep dust out of his eyes. His wife wore a big wide hat covered with a long white chiffon scarf that tied under her chin.

As they passed, the children cheered, not knowing why they cheered, but knowing they were seeing something quite remarkable, with the potential to change life as they knew it. They continued to watch until it drove out of sight, before they continued their race to the river. Stopping on the bank of the Tallahatchie River, they undressed and jumped in the cool water naked.

Over the next hour, those who could swam up and down near the riverbank, while the others had brought homemade soap to wash away the dirt and sweat of the day. Everyone was in the river, except

Leroy, who was on land, sitting by a tree, quietly braiding some twigs. He never liked bathing in the river; there were dangers in the river, like poisonous water moccasins. With no thought about snakes, the children spent more than an hour playing in the cool river water.

CHAPTER **3**

Life in Money

Estella loved going to church—everyone wore their Sunday best. Even for poor folk, she would see them not covered with sweat and dirt from the fields. On Sundays everyone was cleaned up, hair combed back—all dressed up for church. It was the best they would ever look—that is, until you saw them dressed up in their coffin. Today, she was wearing her "good church dress," black patent leather shoes, and clean white socks. Her "church dress" was still a plain blue frock, but unlike her other dresses, was not faded. Her church was a very small wooden building that held only twenty-five members. During the week, this building was the school for Negro children in Money and other surrounding towns and rural areas. As Estella sat in her seat by her family, she wished she was not behind in her studies, but she only attended school a half-day, with little time for learning. After a few hours in school, they would head to the cotton fields, chopping cotton all afternoon, and after that there was work at home in their garden, washing clothes, and cleaning their houses.

But more than anything, she wanted a good education, and hoped they would somehow get newer books and more time in the classroom. The sound of the five-member choir inside the church distracted her thoughts about school. The choir didn't wear robes; they just dressed in their Sunday clothes like everyone else. Their voices were heavenly, making everyone feel that God heard the beautiful songs, blessing everyone in this church. Their singing brought tears to some older women who were fanning themselves.

When the choir stopped, Reverend Lockwood went to his pulpit. He was a stout, short man of forty, dressed in a good suit, looking dignified and stately, not like he looked when he sometimes came by their house for dinner on Sunday and ate lots of their food, fast like a pig. He was a pretty good preacher, but after a half hour of his sermon, she lost interest and began swinging her legs. Her mother, Julia, smacked her legs. Estella sat straight up, making it seem like she was listening to the reverend's sermon. She was happy to finally see the reverend step back and motion for the choir to sing one last hymn.

Coming out of the church and into the bright sunlight, she saw a clear blue sky. Everyone stood out front, not eager to go home, for church was the big event in Money for the whole week. As she stood on the church steps, she could hear the women talk about the sermon…and too often about town gossip. She wasn't interested in their gossip; instead she searched the group of faces to find her Grandfather, but couldn't see him. She walked back into the church trying to find him, walking toward one of the back windows of the church where she saw eight men standing together, including her Grandfather, just outside the church's back entrance.

Exiting the back door, she walked toward her Grandfather, listening quietly as he, Reverend Lockwood, and the other men talked. One very tall and well-dressed man she had seen before on Sundays a number of times. Her Grandfather had told her this man was a porter on the train. She noticed he spoke quite intelligently, not like anyone in Money. Reverend Lockwood and the other men were listening to his every word.

The porter was holding a stack of newspapers. "Now you read this newspaper good, 'cause everything you need to know to advance yourself as Negro people is in the *Chicago Defender* newspaper."

"I read da *Defender*, every word, every time ya bring us that newspaper," said Reverend Lockwood. "We really thank ya fo' using yo porter job on da train ta bring us dis newspaper."

"Don't let white folks know you got this newspaper with all this information to help y'all. It's one of our big secrets," the porter said with a big smile.

The men laughed, overjoyed with talking to the porter. The porter continued, "If you want to make something of your life, want good jobs and good schools for your children, you need to go up North." The porter handed each of the men a newspaper. "We porters bring the *Defender* paper to Negro people all over the South."

Estella saw her Grandfather nodding, as the porter spoke. "Where do you porters get for dese newspapers ta give us free?

Who pays fo' you to give 'em to us?" the reverend asked.

The porter explained, "Mr. Abbott, publisher of the *Chicago Defender*, gives us porters his newspapers for free to take down South. Porters are taking the *Chicago Defender* to big cities, small towns, and rural areas in the South—to Charleston, Atlanta, Florida, Alabama, Arkansas, towns in Texas, all over the South. Mr. Abbott wants you to have them, 'cause he wants to let you all know you need to come up North, get out of this Jim Crow South, with no jobs, few schools, as second-class citizens having to bow to white folks, and get away from the lynchings. The paper is a champion for Negroes; it writes about the lynchings in the South. No other newspaper ever writes 'bout lynchings—like they don't lynch Negros in the South." The men all nodded in agreement, and continued to talk about their hard life in Money—the difficulties they faced just trying to survive and provide for their families. Estella did not completely understand what the porter was saying, but she was very happy about what she did understand, that the newspaper would inform them about how to better their lives.

She dashed away from the men and ran through the large field near the church, enraptured with happiness. She saw several butterflies, each more beautiful than the last. She was amazed at the beauty of butterflies, and other things in nature—like sunsets, the trees, and animals. She wished life was beautiful for everyone and everything. She wished she had a beautiful home, not the shotgun shack where she lived. She wanted pretty clothes and pretty ribbons for her hair. She saw few Negroes with anything pretty at all. Sometimes on Sundays, a woman would show up wearing a pretty new dress, but it was her only dress for church and after seeing that same dress again and again, every Sunday, the beauty was little noticed.

"Estella! Estella! Where are you, gal?" Hearing her mother calling for her, Estella ran back to the church.

CHAPTER 4

Dreams of the North

It was early morning in Money, and the blue sky was beautiful as the sun made its way into the sky. Estella and her mother had been walking for nearly an hour to the Jessup house, which was just four miles away. But the hot sun, with no breeze, made the trip seem longer. The Jessups were sharecroppers who lived on the nearby Wildwood plantation, in a better two-room house—small, but not a shack.

Finally, she saw Roscoe and Rose Jessup, Ruth's parents, setting on their front porch, smiling and waving to them. Julia called out, "Estella just wanted to check on Ruth, after dat snake bite." Julia handed Rose a pie, as a gift. Rose was a big woman with a bright smile and coal-black hair.

"Ruth doin' just fine," replied Roscoe, a tall, thin, light-skinned man with salt and pepper hair, smoking a corn pipe. Ruth came to the door and waved, smiling, looking recovered, but a little weak.

"Estella, there's Ruth!" Rose pointed out, "So, ya see, she doin' fine, like I told ya she was."

Estella was very pleased that her actions to help Ruth had worked.

"Julia, ya hear what happen down in Yazoo City Tuesday? You know they done lynched a Negro man fo' bumpin' into a white man. I'm telling ya, it gettin' worse..." Roscoe said, shaking his head.

"Sho ain't gettin' any better. Dey wanna lynch a Negro fo'any lil' thing."

"It making life hard to swallow, gotta live like dis. Did y'all hear the Butlers done moved North to Detroit last month, with their chil'ren? So dey can have a good life ahead fo' dem now..." Rose added.

"Mr. and Mrs. Butler can have a good life ahead fo' dem too in da North. Up North, at least there be somewhere in dis world where a Negro has a chance." Julia added.

"Yes, da North and South, it be different as day and night." Roscoe replied.

Rose laughed, "Dere is schools in Mississippi fo' Negro chil'ren, here and there. Ruth's on her way to Greenwood and goin' to get a certificate fo' eighth grade. It be a good school, teachin' mo than that lil' school round here. So it's good Estella cured dat snake bite, 'cause Ruth goin' to be a teacher."

Estella looked at the Jessups' nice flower garden as she listened. And she listened well. *She wondered if she could ever get a good education, and if she would ever see the North.* But for ten year- old Estella, the thought of seeing the North was too distant; she quickly pushed it from her mind...though she hoped somehow she could get a proper education. Saying goodbye to the Jessups, Estella and her mother made their way down the road for the long walk home and their long day of hard work.

After toiling in the cotton fields from dawn to dusk, there was little or no time for play. Five acres of the plantation were set aside for the sharecroppers to use as their own. The Reynolds shared the land with several other families, where they planted vegetables to eat and sell, and a flower garden to attract bees to make honey. But in the end, there was no real money for the sharecropper, only for the one who owned the land and reaped nearly all the money from the crops grown. Paul didn't buy supplies on credit from the general store in Money. That way, by the end of the year, he would not be in debt to the man who owned the land, like most sharecroppers.

There was always something to do, including milking the cow, and planting and harvesting a wide variety of vegetables. Today, she was making soap in the big No. 10 tub, and then she joined her mother to chop and pull weeds. It was especially hard work in the heat of the day, but neither Julia nor Estella stopped for a moment. As they continued to work, a wagon came along the road and stopped along the roadside. A tall, dark Negro woman jumped down, waving to them as the wagon pulled away. It was Aunt Mattie, Julia's sister, who had been working hard all day at a white family's house. Mattie walked over to Julia and Estella, carrying a bag. They stopped working as Mattie pulled a dress from a bag.

"Look what Miss Betsy give me today," Mattie told them. "Right nice dress; you get along well with white folks, Mattie." "Ain't nothing wrong with people gettin' along, Julia."

"I don't like 'em—don't think I ever will like 'em…. Don't like how dey treat us…!"

Estella was surprised to learn that her mother did not care for white people; she had noticed that her mother was often silent in their presence, saying nothing, and not smiling.

"I wanna go North," her mother added.

"What you goin to do up North, Julia? Ya don't know 'bout da North; and ya don't know one soul in da North."

"Better than here, even better than cleaning dey house and smilin' at ya and payin' ya almost nothin'!"

"Ya better not let white folk hear ya talkin' like dat," Mattie warned her sister.

Julia wiped the sweat from her brow, saying, "I'm gonna make a nice cold lemonade when I go in da house."

With her chores finished, Estella rubbed lard on her hands as lotion. She strolled across the field where Leroy was toiling with a mule-driven plow, saying, "Leroy, you ain't movin' dat plow straight. I'd move it straight and even...."

"You think ya know everything, gal. But ya ain't never plowed with no mule!"

Estella had not, but she figured she could do a better job of it than Leroy; she laughed. The two suddenly turned, when they heard a scream. It was loud, near their shack, coming from the outhouse. Julia came fleeing from the outhouse, pulling up her drawers.

"A snake...a snake in da outhouse!" she cried out.

Quickly Paul picked up a hoe and ran to the outhouse; seeing the snake slither toward him, he hit it hard several times, killing it. Knowing the snake was now dead, Leroy and Estella ran to the outhouse, trying to console Julia, who was still upset and crying. As everyone returned to the house, Estella stayed outside and headed to the nearby woods. At the edge of the trees, she stopped, looked down, and saw a mound with ants all around it, going in and out of the mound. The ants were working together like little soldiers, in harmony, peacefully building their ant homes, and *she wondered why people didn't do the same.* Hearing footsteps, she looked up seeing her

Grandfather walking into the woods—this seemed to be something he did a lot, if not every day. Estella called out, "Papa, can I go in da woods wid ya today?"

"No, Estella. I want ta go dere alone… to rest my mind." "Rest yo mind? Why you need to do that?"

"Ya know I told ya, it's 'bout resting yo mind in peace and quiet." Estella didn't understand. It was getting dark now; and as her Grandfather continued into the woods, she knew it was time to get home. As she entered the house, she smelled chicken frying, which she loved, for fried chicken smelled as good as it tasted. She immediately joined her mother sitting at the table shelling fresh peas from the garden for dinner. Her mother's big bed was in a small room by the front door, with little else in the room, except a table, mismatched chairs, a cabinet, an old four-legged stove, and smaller beds on the other side of the room behind a curtain. Their home was a worn out shack with old furniture, but it was home, and it was cozy. Estella enjoyed family dinners with her brother and two baby sisters. Almost every evening, her Grandfather's sister Mandy and Aunt Mattie would stop. Her Grandfather always came by, just in time for dinner. The only missing family member was her brother, Walter, who was just eleven months younger than Estella. He was in the back room of the shack, sick, and he slept much of the day.

After supper, it was dark and the fireplace was lit keeping it warm and giving off light. Three coal oil lamps also burned, which started with a small flame that soon glowed brightly lighting the room quite well. Estella's younger sisters, Laura and baby Elizabeth, sat in the middle of the floor playing with a raggedy rag doll.

At the table, Leroy was cracking open and quickly eating pecans and walnuts. The fresh nuts had come from their own trees, and for right now, Estella's world seemed perfect as she grabbed a couple of pecans from the table. She turned to her Grandfather, who sat at the head of the table, and asked, "What ya reading, Papa?"

"The *Defender* newspaper, a second time."

Julia laughed. "Who you foolin', Paul? It just take him all day to read a little bit!"

"Sho ain't no opportunities here in Money." Leroy complained.

> *"There be lotsa Negroes, thousands even, goin' from Mississippi up North to Chicago. After slavery, white folks tried ta force Negroes to stay and be sharecroppers, working in the fields. But there ain't too many young folks that will sign on to be a sharecropper after dey done seen how it is just another way of slavery. If 'n ya work the white man's land, he just gives ya credit at the general store. At the end of da year ya always owe him, and ya find yo'self stuck working in dem fields forever, like slavery,"* Paul told them.

"I heard ya kin get jobs in Chicago payin' five dollars a week or mo." Leroy added.

"Now that's money, boy! Sho do beat pickin' cotton!"

"From da pictures in da newspaper, women dress real pretty. They got pretty hats, dresses, shoes. Churches wrote up in dat newspaper got lots of church members," Julia said.

"Everything's big there, 'cordin' to the paper," said Paul.

"But is dat true? You believe all dat newspaper writin' bout?" questioned Mattie.

"Look, I talked ta people dat been there and come back ta pick up relatives. Dey say it is all true, and mo than dat. Chicago is a big city; dey got lots of business there and jobs fo' everyone; it is all true." Paul replied, laying down the newspaper.

Estella picked up the paper and sat on the floor looking at the pictures and advertisements. She had not looked at it before, and was amazed by what she saw. She would recall pictures in the newspaper for days. The paper was overwhelming, and Estella put it down after a few pages, wanting to read and absorb it all, a few pages a day. She stepped outside onto the porch, glad that she had used the outhouse before dinner, now scared to go in there after dark to maybe face a snake. Next to the shack, she saw Leroy taking his bath outside in a tub. This is where he wanted to bathe—not the river, but at home, and outside. Julia let the young boy bathe the way he wanted.

Estella's thoughts were not on Leroy scrubbing himself, but on the hundreds of fireflies lighting the sky. Then she gazed at the dark sky glittering with vivid stars, so bright it seemed she could reach out and touch them, as she recalled the pictures in the newspaper.

Leroy was finished bathing. He had dressed and was heading into the house, when Julia met him at the door, telling him, "we all out of flour ta cook pancakes fo' breakfast! I need you and Estella to run to the store and get me some flour. Go quick, 'cause it be late!"

Julia handed Leroy some money, and he and Estella set out down the dark road. After a short walk they entered a remote wooded road, taking a shortcut.

"Leroy, Mama didn't tell ya to take no shortcut." "She said go quick, gal, and dis be da quickest way."

Choosing to take the shortcut to the store meant it was only a half mile walk. But the road was very dark and they had never taken the shortcut at night before. Although there was a full moon out and thousands of bright starts, it was hard to see for all the trees on the remote road; making the road seem strangely eerie at night.

"What do ya think bout dat newspaper?"

"Huh? Let's walk faster, gal—it's gettin' too dark!"

Estella realized her brother was getting very nervous about the dark. She didn't really like it either. They began to walk as fast as they could, staying close to the bush.

Leroy finally replied, "Da *Chicago Defender*, yeah. It sounds real good. I know we gotta get good work and we gotta go where that good work be. But Chicago is so far away gal."

"Look, Leroy!" Estella pointed ahead of them. The two stopped and saw a bright glow about sixty feet up the road; it looked like torches. As they walked closer, they could make out over a dozen men dressed in white costumes with pointed hoods, on horses, holding torches. Leroy and Estella stepped closer to the bush.

Estella whispered, "Let's get in da bush and watch dem. I wanna take a better look...."

"No! That be the Ku Klux Klan; dey string up Negro folks! Let's get away from here! Get home! Quick!" Leroy urged.

The torch fires up the road blazed wildly as Leroy and Estella turned and fled, running faster than they ever had run to get back home. The next week, as they took another shortcut through the woods, the November afternoon sun shone brightly through the leaves of the tall oak trees. Wearing light jackets, Estella and Leroy walked along, crushing the multicolored autumn leaves on the forest floor; enjoying the cool fall day.

Estella said, "We makin' good money deliverin' some of Uncle Leamon's jams to people in town. He sells all kinds of jams—grape, apple, peach, cherry jams, sealin' dem in mason jars and dey preserved fo' da winter...."

Leroy snarled, "He's givin' us a penny a jar—we just delivered, when he sells dose jams fo' a dime a jar. And Uncle Leamon don't make da jam; women round da fields make it and he give 'em two cents a jar."

"He's smart," she replied.

"Real smart; and Papa smart too! I'm gone tell ya a secret…." "A secret?"

"Yeah, Papa got a secret garden here in da woods, and Mr. Carson don't know 'bout it. Papa sells da vegetables he grow to make extra money— now that be the secret."

"That ain't no secret, gal! I knows Papa got dat garden to make some money. A man's gotta make money. White folks make it hard for us, and you have to find a way ta make some…."

Estella looked around, startled. "Shhh…" She whispered. Suddenly, they saw three white men walking toward them, arguing. Estella and Leroy quickly ducked behind a tree, hiding as they listened. They recognized the men—it was the Sheriff from Money, Mr. Carson, and his cousin that lived in the area.

"I tell ya it's not mine," Mr. Carson told the Sheriff.

"It's on your land and these woods be on your land. If 'n my cousin here found a moonshine still makin' liquor on your land, ya must be da one makin' it." The Sheriff told Mr. Carson.

"I ain't makin' no moonshine, I tell ya…!"

"Then who is makin' it, Carson?" asked the Sheriff.

"How da hell I know? Dese woods are big, anybody could be comin' here doin' dis."

"Well, we know it ain't no nigger 'round here doin' this, cause that moonshine still is the best I done seen in the county and can't no po' dumb nigger make or run it." The Sheriff said. "Well, I ain't runnin' it, if I don't own it."

"We gotta take ya in fo' mo questions, Carson. But if you get a little money, maybe I can forget about it."

"I tell ya it ain't mine; I'm gonna talk to my lawyer."

Estella and Leroy saw the three men get in the Sheriff's car.

Estella exclaimed, "Mr. Carson makin' moonshine!"

"Shhh—let's not tell anybody 'bout no white man gettin' in trouble. Negroes best use their brains good in da South, or any big or little thing can get us in trouble," Leroy whispered. The two children continued through the forest.

"I think Mr. Carson's makin' money—makin' moon shine on dat side and cheatin' us sharecroppers."

"Is he in lots of trouble, Leroy?"

"Dat moonshine still is on his land. Yup, he in trouble, if 'n he don't pay off the Sheriff," Leroy said.

23

CHAPTER 5

He Shot Her!

It seemed that every morning, Estella was one of the first to wake up, even before the rooster crowed. Sharing a bed with her little sisters, Laura and Elizabeth, she made sure not to disturb them and was the first to touch her bare feet to the cold wooden floor. The fire in the fireplace had died; she grabbed a few small twigs, a box of matches, and an iron poker to rebuild a fire. She could smell the bacon her mother was already cooking. She dressed quickly and walked out to the kitchen.

"Mornin', Mama—you want me to help?"

"Well hello, sleepy head—yes, please pump some water in them buckets, so I can put them on the stove. We need to boil some water to wash this mornin'. The bacon is almost done; we can eat after we fill the buckets."

"Yes, Mama." Estella replied, feeling her stomach growl. Everyone got up early this next morning, just after sunrise.

Estella washed up, it was Sunday, a wonderful day because there was no work in cotton fields or on the farm. She loved Sundays; going to church was her favorite day. They would set out for church

24

at eight o'clock in the morning and sometimes did not return back home until five o'clock in the afternoon.

As the family rode toward the church, Estella could not help thinking about her brother, Walter. Walter was always laughing and singing church songs with her each Sunday. He had died last winter; while other family members seemed to be over his death, she still felt the pain. Walter was eleven months older than she; they grew up together, worked and played together all her life. But now he was gone, taken away from them far too early. She knew nothing could bring Walter back.

As they passed along the road, surrounded by fruit trees, the branches hung within arm's reach of some very big, ripe apples. As their wagon passed an apple tree, Estella reached up and grabbed an apple and bit into it.

Julia pointed out, "Ya know, it's a shame we don't have decent schools fo' our children. We just got one-room shacks fo' schools, with them torn old books that white kids done used."

"Some places in da South there ain't schools fo' Negro chil'ren." Paul said.

Julia complained, "I notice how Negro teachers finish only eighth grade to become a teacher, but white teachers dat teach white chi'ren have to finish college. White chi'ren got nice schools, with new books and desks!"

"Why, Mama?" Estella asked. "Why? Why? Why? Why white chi'ren's teachers finish college, but Negro chi'ren's teachers only finish eighth grade?"

Her Grandfather laughed. "That gal always askin' why? Just learn the best you can, and get as much education as you kin, gal, like I told ya."

Aunt Mandy said, "Estella, you gonna learn someday why. I guess dey scared of us as free people, cause dey sho wanna hold us down. It is so wrong, so bad how dey treatin' us."

"Dey wants to always to hold us down forever. We'll pull up some day… somehow," added Julia. They turned onto another dirt road, passing a deplorably run down farm. While the house was pretty large, it was not kept up by whoever lived there. The house needed painting and many repairs. And the whole farm was filthy and looked a mess, with no garden, only dirt. Piles of rubbish lay throughout the front yard.

"Dat outhouse stinks," said Mandy.

A white farmer, about forty, was standing on the road, and turned to them. He stepped before their wagon, and raised his hands to stop them. Julia pulled on the reins, stopping the wagon just feet from the farmer. He stood in front of the wagon with his hands on his hips and a mean look on his face. Glancing over at Mandy, he pointed at her and shouted, "I got somethin' fo' ya—y'all wait here!" The man ran to his house, less than twenty feet from the road, slamming the front door behind him.

"I wonda what he got fo' me," said Mandy, as they all sat curiously, waiting.

In less than three minutes, the farmer stepped outside onto the porch steps. He quickly lifted a rifle and aimed it at Mandy; and pulled the trigger. The sound of the gunshot echoed through the air. Estella covered her ears, turning to look at her Grandfather— she noticed Mandy falling back into her mother's lap. They were all shocked to see blood flowing from Mandy's chest. Paul started to jump down from the wagon, outraged by this horrific act. Before he could move, Julia grabbed his arm, trying to restrain him from any future danger.

Estella held Mandy in her arms, hearing her Grandfather say, "The low-down scoundrel done killed my sister! I'm gonna kill him!"

Julia cried out, "You know you can't...Paul Reynolds!! You know ya can't kill dat white man, 'cause ya know what dey gone do to ya!" Paul knew she was right; he would have to control his outrage to save his own life and the lives of his other family members. But he was too stunned to move. Julia grabbed Mandy from Estella's arms, holding Mandy close as she took her last breath. Seeing Paul sulking in rage, Julia looked around terrified, and took the reins, slapping the old mule as hard as she could. This time he ran down the road, faster than ever.

"I know I gotta get out of da South, befo' things comes to a bad end fo' me," Paul added.

Estella felt a great chill; she could not believe what she had just witnessed. In cold blood, for no reason but a simple, obvious, minor comment, and he killed her. *Why do white people hate us? She wondered.* This day, Estella was learning how awful it was in the South. Stepping aside to let them pass first and waiting after they jumped before Negroes in line, she had managed to accept, but to kill like that, and the lynchings for small things Negro people said and did, which white people did not like, was horrendous, uncivilized, and hellish. It was dawning on her that life in the South was nearly unbearable for Negroes.

She wished she had not seen something so cruel and evil as that, and she did not want to live somewhere to witness anything so dreadful. Hot heavy tears rushed from her eyes, as her mind raced pondering how one day she was going to get away from here. She thought, *People don't treat people right here. Why do I have to be treated less than a human being? Why do I have to step aside for white folks coming down the road? Why do I have to work in the cotton fields, and I can't go to school for a full day? Why do we have to die for no reason?*

"Papa, what we gonna tell the Sheriff about how Mandy got killed?" Estella asked.

"Well now, y'all know if we tell him a white man shot her, I don't know if he be in the Klan, and bad things could come our way. I think we best say we heard a bang, and she fell dead—maybe a man was huntin' in the woods."

"Yes, Paul, that there is a good idea!" Julia said.

Paul shouted, "We got to take Mandy's body into Greenwood, so the Sheriff don't think we done killed her!" Taking the reins from Julia, with all his strength and anger, he hit the reins harder on the mule's backside, making Estella almost fall from the wagon seat. Finally, when they reached Greenwood, Paul and Leroy went into the Sheriff's office to tell him how Mandy had been shot and killed as they passed some woods on the way from church.

Estella and Julia waited nervously outside. Within minutes, the Sheriff, Paul, and Leroy stepped outside and walked to the back of the wagon where Mandy's body lay, her hair and chest covered with blood. They all watched as the Sheriff examined her body. "How I know y'all boys telling me the truth about what happened to his here gal?" Turning Mandy's body over, he looked into the large wound that carried through to the other side.

"Y'all need to come back in my office to answers some questions 'bout this," the Sheriff added.

Fear ran through Julia and Estella—what was the Sheriff going to do with her Grandfather and brother? As they waited, they watched helplessly as the three men disappeared into the office.

For nearly two hours, Julia tried to comfort her daughter's fears. "It gonna be all right, gal—you just stop worrying."

Just then the office door opened, with Paul and Leroy walking toward the wagon. "What the Sheriff goin' to do, Paul?" Julia asked. "He ain't goin to do nothin'! He only know what we tell him, if we all say the same thing!"

Estella was shocked for the second time that day. *How could this happen? And why? It was always the same answer....because the South was just that way. So what if it was just another Negro dead in the South?*

Once again, tears streamed down her face, as her Grandfather and brother boarded the wagon. In silence, Paul turned the wagon around, and together the family rode on back to Money. The only sound came from Julia, who kept sighing, "Why, dear Lord? Why?" The following Sunday was going to be the day of Mandy's funeral. Paul had taken his sister's body to the undertaker the night she was shot. Now the family dressed and ate quietly.

Julia stood at the kitchen window, looking out to see a gray cloudy sky, "Sometimes I think some people have no feelings," she said in a soft voice.

Paul answered, "They can take someone's life, like it ain't nothin'!"

"Lord have mercy....when will all this stop," Julia asked with tears in her eyes. Estella knew there was nothing else to say.

"Y'all better be gettin' ready; Reverend Lockwood goin' to start the service early today," Paul told them.

As the family rode to the church, Estella continued to think about how Mandy had been killed. As the family filed into the church, Paul added, "I don't want to go in...but I got to."

Standing at the coffin, Julia said, "She look so peaceful."

A few minutes later everyone took a seat in the pews near the front of the church, as Reverend Lockwood walked past the coffin and up to the pulpit, saying, "Let the service begin." Everyone was shocked—there was a big smile on his face.

"I know you think this smile on my face is out of place on such a sad day. But today is not a day to be sad. It is a day to be glad. Our Sister Mandy is at peace. I am smiling because she ain't goin' to pick cotton in the hot sun no mo! She ain't goin to be disrespected no mo! She ain't goin' to be poor no mo! She ain't goin to say ...yes ma'am and yes sir, no mo because of the color of someone's skin no mo!

She ain't goin' to see no mo Negroes hanging from a tree! If only our world would be a place of peace, love, respect, and understanding. 'cause Sister Mandy is in a place of peace and love!"

Everyone nodded, knowing the reverend was right, and suddenly Paul and his family felt at peace too. The reverend motioned for the choir to sing another hymn as the coffin was carried out the church's front doors and to the small cemetery behind the church. As the four men gently lowered the coffin into the ground, the reverend said a prayer. Just as he finished, the sun came from behind the clouds, filling the sky with light. Pointing to the sky, Reverend Lockwood said, "Sister Mandy just got a new home!"

CHAPTER **6**

High Water

It was the spring of 1927 and the Tallahatchie River was getting higher every day, covering more and more ground. Over the past few days the family had watched as the water started to encircle their shack. In some places, pools of water left fish washed up and trapped inside small puddles. Today, taking advantage of the situation, Paul, Estella, and Leroy were out trying to catch their dinner for the night. As they walked, they noticed a small ditch, filled with dozens of fish, trapped and splashing.

"Go get some rocks, Leroy, to hold dem fish in this here ditch," shouted their Grandfather.

"There is some big ones in here," Leroy yelled back. "Mama gonna love all these here fish. I see some catfish, sunfish, and bass." "If the river gets any bigger; there ain't gonna be nowhere to cook 'em," his sister told him.

By the time Estella got out of bed the next morning, the water that had swelled into their house, and into her bedroom. She stepped down from her bed and her feet got wet.

"The house is flooding, Mama! It's all inside the bedroom and gettin' deeper!" Her mother Julia jumped out of bed only to step into six inches of water. "Get the babies out here!" she yelled.

"Where we goin'?" the frightened Leroy asked.

"To your Uncle's house up on the hill. Quick, boy—help carry these babies! Hold hands and run, before dis here river carry us and dis house away!"

It didn't take long before the escaping family noticed the water had turned to mud and mud to damp ground. Estella stood at the top of the small hill; turning toward her family, her face full of fear, she yelled, "Stop!"

"What's wrong?" Leroy yelled as he moved up the hill toward his sister.

"The water is too deep on the other side!"

"What you talkin' bout, gal?" He realized that the river had cut a big channel between the hill and where they stood. "That water could be ten or fifteen feet deep," he shouted.

"How we gonna cross the water," his mother asked, holding his baby sister Elizabeth in her arms with five-year-old Laura holding on to her dress hem.

"We gotta cross now, Mama; the water be comin' up behind us too!"

Estella shouted, "I can swim across and get help!"

Before her mother could answer, they saw Uncle Leamon coming down the hill toward the channel pulling a big tin tub behind him with a small rope tied to one of the handles. The hill was steep and muddy causing him to slip toward the edge of the rising water. "Hold on! I'll bring this here tub over to you," Leamon called out as he waded into the cool water at the bottom of the hill. He found the water was not as deep as it appeared. "This water is only up to my waist, I recon if y'all hold hands you can make it across okay."

As Leamon pulled the tub behind him through the fast moving water, Estella and Leroy reached out their hands to help their Uncle as he got closer to them. "We can put the chil'ren in dis here tub." Leroy said.

"That's a good idea," Julia told him.

Just then Leamon took Julia by the arm helping her to cross the water, while Leroy and Estella placed Elizabeth and Laura in the tub. They used the rope to pull the tub out into the rushing water; being shorter than their Uncle, the water came almost up to their shoulders. Estella stopped pulling the tub and put her hand high in the air to tell Leroy to stop—just in time to see a long water moccasin moving toward them.

She knew her brother was very afraid of snakes, saying, "don't move Leroy! That snake will pass us, no need to be scared!"

Leroy watched as the snake slithered away and finally disappeared into the light fog that was beginning to roll up from the water's surface. Knowing they were out of danger for a moment, they continued to pull the tub behind them toward the opposite shore, with the two small children safe inside. Within minutes, although it seemed much longer, Leamon was able to run out and help everyone ashore.

Cold and shivering, Leamon said, "we better get up this here hill to the house fo' we all catch the death of pneumonia!" They were all too exhausted to say a word. Leamon, Julia and Estella held hands as Leroy carried little Elizabeth, while Laura walked behind them. The family struggled to walk up the muddy hill to Leamon's house, just twenty-five feet above the water's edge.

Just outside the house, Leamon grabbed two pieces of firewood that was stacked under the overhang, "We got to make a big fire in the fireplace and in the stove. Y'all better get out of them wet clothes right now!"

Placing two logs on top of the red-hot coals in the fireplace, Leamon struggled to get a fire going with the wet logs. He handed Estella two more pieces of wood so she could put them into the big black pot-belly stove in the corner of the living room. Julia and her daughters went into the small bedroom near the back of the house to take off their wet clothes, while Leroy and Leamon undressed in the living room. The family was soon standing before the fireplace, with dry clothing—getting warm and thankful for making it back safely. Estella wandered over to the small window next to the door; she wanted to see if the water was still rising. Instead, she noticed something that looked like a long log coming down the stream, but something about this log was different. She continued to watch as the log stopped at the edge of the water and suddenly started moving again on its own—*it seemed to be walking,* she thought.

"Hey y'all! Come look—I see something I ain't seen before!" Estella pointed to something outside. Leroy and Julia ran to the widow, trying to see what Estella was pointing at.

"Well now, that there looks like an alligator," shouted Leroy. "How an alligator get here?" Julia asked.

"The flood musta washed him up with the high water," Leamon answered, looking out the window. "Y'all better stay in the house—that thing can kill ya!"

"Where you going?" Estella asked her Uncle as he headed for the door. "Don't go out there!"

"I got to go, and I'll tell you why when I come back—come on, boy, I need you to go with me."

Leroy was shocked to hear his Uncle's words. "You want me to go with you?" he asked Leamon.

"Come on, boy, and stop talkin' back—if I didn't want you to go, why would I ask ya?" With that, Leamon opened the front door. He whispered, "Shhh, Leroy, quiet—don't make a sound, or we goin' to lose him."

"That's okay with me!" Leroy replied in a low voice, peeking out from behind his Uncle.

"Hush, boy…" his Uncle whispered again. Moving quickly to the side of the house, Leamon found a long piece of rope from the tub that had been used to pull the family across the rising water. He made a loop on one end as Leroy looked on.

"What you goin' to do with that?" The boy whispered.

"Just you wait and see. I need to climb up that tree over yonder. You best stop watching with your mouth and see with your eyes Leroy! Go cuts me down one of them hams inside the smokehouse, boy!"

Leamon handed over his pocket knife, saying, "Don't make no noise—get goin'."

Leroy walked slowly and quietly toward the small wooden smoke house his Grandfather Paul had built a few years ago. He opened the door and the smell of smoked ham came rushing out. He was trying to figure out what his Uncle was going to do with the ham and rope. Reaching for the smallest ham, he cut it down, closed the door behind him, and walked back toward his Uncle, the alligator, and the river. *Leroy wondered—what if that alligator took off after them. He didn't know what might happen.*

Reaching his Uncle's side, Leroy handed him the small ham and waited as his Uncle took the knife from him and cut a small hole in the middle of the ham. Leamon then pulled the end of the rope through the hole he had cut in the meat. *What is he doin'? The young boy wondered.* He knew the ham would make a good meal for the family.

"Don't just stand there, boy," his Uncle said. "Help me get up that tree."

Looking over at the alligator, Leroy answered, "Who—me?" "Boy, I ain't got all day; that thing goin' to move any time now!"

Leamon started toward the big brown oak tree that stood near the edge of the water. The only good thing about all this—Leroy thought—was that the tree his Uncle wanted him to climb was far away from the alligator.

Estella and Julia were still watching, with fear and concern imprinted on their faces. They could see Leamon high up in the tree, looking for a big heavy branch; he quickly dropped the looped end over the branch and wrapped the rope around the branch two times with the other end tied to the ham. Then he placed it just behind the loop, hoping that the gator would put his head through the loop to get to the ham. The knot he had tied above would slip and tighten once the gator went for the meat.

As they watched, *Estella and Julia wondered why anyone would want to catch that ugly thing—and what would you do with the gator.* His trap now in place, Leamon slowly climbed down the tree to get his hunting rifle.

"Okay, Leroy—don't just stand there; get movin', and be quiet!" Keeping an eye on the gator, Leroy noticed that it had not moved much—only about a foot or so. Moving very slowly across the yard, he never took his eyes off the gator. But if it did move much, the boy was ready to run as fast as he could to the safety of their little shack. Once inside, Leroy quickly found where Leamon kept his rifle that Grandpa Paul gave him some years ago.

Walking toward the front door, Estella followed her brother, looking very puzzled over what she had seen from the window. "What are y'all doin' out yonder?"

"We tryin' to catch that gator!" "For what," Julia asked.

"I don't know—ask Uncle Leamon," Leroy replied, as he walked out the door and toward the big oak tree.

"Hurry up, boy—just be quiet..shhhh," his Uncle whispered, placing his finger to his lips.

Leamon took the rifle from Leroy, and tossed a piece of the ham toward the gator. Seeing and smelling the meat, the gator raised his head slightly, and inched forward.

"We better get out of here," Leroy whispered to Leamon. "Walk, don't run," Leamon responded, "or that thing may think we taste better than that there ham!"

Moving slowly across the slippery muddy yard to the front door of the small shack, they both kept an eye on the big creature, which was still making his way to the chunk of ham Leamon had thrown. When they reached the shack, they looked back to see the gator open his mouth and gulp down the first piece of meat, then lunge toward the second hunk of ham.

"Close the door," Estella yelled, as her brother and Uncle stepped inside, "I don't want that thing to get in this here house!" Slamming the door behind them, everyone ran to the front window, just as the gator went for the bait.

"Boy, look at that," Julia said, pointing to the gator as it splashed water high into the air, rolling its large body over and over, making the rope wrap around it with every roll.

"It worked," shouted Leamon, "I think we got him!" Still carrying the rifle, he opened the door, moved past the women, and motioned to Leroy to follow him. The gator was splashing even harder, trying to escape. Then a growl, like nothing Leamon had ever heard, came from the beast.

"What if that thing gets loose," Estella asked. "Y'all better be careful," Julia added.

They crossed the front yard, moving back toward the spot where the gator was still struggling to get free, his efforts turning the muddy water into white foam. "Just look at that," Leamon said, "we got him good!"

Just as he raised his rifle, a loud voice called out, "What you boys got there?"

It was Mr. Carson and his son Chip, coming down the path from his house near the top of the hill. Mr. Carson was a tall redheaded man, who ran the Wildwood Plantation for Mr. Delwood. Mr. Carson's son Chip was short for ten years old, chubby and redheaded like his father. He looked much older, maybe fifteen or so, and was known to be a mean child.

"Don't kill that gator—we need to keep him alive. He ain't gonna be worth nothin' if y'all kill 'em! You boys better hope that rope holds," Mr. Carson yelled.

Before Leamon could respond, Mr. Carson shouted to his son, "Chip, go up to the house and load that dog cage on to the wagon—we goin' to need it to round up this here gator."

Pointing at Leroy, Mr. Carson yelled to his son, "Take this here boy with ya. You'll need his help putting that cage on the wagon." Chip and Leroy ran up the hill, while Estella and Julia looked on as the men tried to capture the thing in the water.

"You gals better get back in the house," Leamon said, "That thing could get loose."

Estella took one last look over at boiling water, and motioned to her mother. "Let's go—he's right 'bout that thing, Mama. That thing is tryin' to wiggle out the rope!"

"Well now, Leamon, don't you know you might get two dollars and fifty cent fo' dis here gator?"

"Don't worry, Mr. Carson. We gonna pull that gator in—just wait and see."

"I wonder what taking them so long to get that cage down here?" Before he could answer, Leamon saw Chip and Leroy riding toward them in the Carson's wagon, pulled by an old gray mule with the rusty dog cage in the back of the wagon.

"We need to get up in that tree and get hold on the end of the rope so we can put him in the cage," Leamon said.

"But when we cut him loose from the tree, we all better be pulling on the rope, fo' that thing swim off rope and all." Mr. Carson told them.

Chip and Leroy moved toward the oak tree, but Mr. Carson called them back, saying, "Holding on to that rope is man's work. You boys get that cage down and open that door real wide, hear me?"

Leamon walked over to the tree, with Mr. Carson following him. Reaching the limb where the rope was; he untied one end, and immediately felt a powerful pull on the other end. "How am I supposed to hold this rope and get down at the same time?"

"Just throw down the end of the rope, Leamon," Mr. Carson called up to him, "so we can pull that gator in."

Leamon dropped the rope down to ground, Leroy catching it as it dropped. Chip and Mr. Carson quickly grabbed the rope, too. By now the gator was tired and was moving much slower. Just as Leroy, Leamon, Chip, and Mr. Carson started to pull on the rope, the gator came to life pulling, turning, jumping, rolling, and snapping.

"Hold on, boys!" Mr. Carson called out, as a tug of war began. For the next thirty minutes they hung on and finally were able to drag the gator from the water and place it in the open cage. "You boys done a good job; I'll pay you a bit in a day or two. Let's get this here cage up on the wagon."

"This cage is heavy," Chip said, as all four of them tried to pick up the big cage with the gator inside—it was too heavy.

"We goin' to need them boards over yonder to get this thing in the wagon," Leamon told them. With that, Chip and Leroy ran toward the house; they picked up two long wooden boards near the house, and brought them back to the rear of the wagon. Placing the boards upon the back of the wagon, they pushed the cage up the boards until it came to rest inside the wagon.

Estella had watched the whole thing from the front of house, wanting it all to be over. *Why did they want to catch that ugly thing, anyway? She wondered.*

Paul Reynolds had been at his sister Mattie's house as the water rose and began to swallow up the land like some big slow-moving monster. Paul, Mattie, and her husband Joseph stood in the front yard of their house, watching as the gator was being captured, hoping nothing bad would happen. Estella and Julia came running toward Leroy and Leamon to see if they were all right after the fight with the gator.

Over the next two days, the water and mud made it hard for everyone to get around; even the chickens lived on top of the chicken coop, and their two cows had to stand in mud more than four inches deep. Thick mud also covered the floor of their home, from the front door to the rear door. Everything was wet, and smelled musty. The only good thing about the mud in the house was the cracks in the floor where mud could be washed down with water and a broom. Estella knew there would be a lot of work cleaning up the mess the flood left behind. It took weeks of back-breaking work to get things cleaned up. But all in all, after four weeks of pushing, washing down, and shoveling mud, the only thing left of the flood was the damp musty smell. That smell, Estella and Julia could not wash away no matter how much they cleaned.

Estella and Leroy took a walk down to the riverbank after the water receded, looking down in a hole near the river's edge. Estella cried out, "look at all them fish!"

Leroy bent over to see about a hundred fish in the low spot—all kinds of bass, sun fish, perch, and catfish. The low spot was about six feet long, ten feet wide, and almost four feet deep.

"Go tell Papa bout the fish in the hole," Leroy told Estella. Excited about all the fish, Estella ran to the back of the shack where her Grandfather was washing down the side of the shack with a bucket of water and a brush.

"Papa come look what we done found—some fish!"

"Gal, what you talkin bout?"

"Come see...Papa!" With that, Paul and Estella started down toward the river.

"What y'all got here?" Paul asked, as he reached the low spot where the fish were trapped.

"We done found a whole bunch of fish, Papa—see all them fish?" Estella asked, standing next to her Grandfather.

"We can just jump in this here hole and put them in the big tub." Leroy said.

"Not so fast," Paul told Leroy. "If 'n we take them out now, we need to get some ice, then clean and cook 'em right now. We got too many. If 'n we take just a few out at a time, we can tell Mattie, Leamon, and the others, so they can come get some fish in the next few days."

Paul knew that the water was deep enough for the fish to live for about a week. Over the next few days, family members and neighbors came to the low spot to get fresh fish. Estella and Leroy got tired of cleaning fish, and their mother got tired of cooking them. To Estella, the fish in the low spot made up for the five chickens lost in the flood.

CHAPTER 7

The Picnic

All year fourteen year old Estella had been waiting for the annual sharecroppers' picnic. More than one hundred sharecroppers and their families flocked to the picnic grounds. They came from all the big plantations around Money to eat and have a good time. The picnic was held on a clearing in the woods of Wildwood plantation, by the river. By noon the picnic grounds was filled with children jumping rope and participating in races, while adults cooked, ate, and talked to sharecroppers from other plantations. Most of them, they hadn't seen in months. The men unloaded the wagons, while the women prepared the food. Paul and Leroy unloaded the pots and pans of food from their wagon, handing them to Julia, Estella, and Mattie.

"Y'all better move this food to the tables or the picnic will be over before you get there," Paul said, laughing.

Small tables made of wood were side by side, creating long tables covered with food—from chicken to ham and every kind of pie and cake. Pastor Lockwood was already sitting at a table by a tree, eating corn on the cob. Several older men sat with him, including Uncle

Bennie, one of Paul's several brothers. Bennie was taller than his brother and always dressed nicely. Today he wore a beige suit, white shirt and shoes that matched his suit. He talked as the men at the table listened intently and often laughed at Bennie's long colorful tales about making money, buying and selling things.

There were races with adults and races for children; everyone was eating and having fun. For the most part, the women sat at the end of the table talking about who made the best pie, or sewed the prettiest dress. Estella felt great joy today, and she loved the new red and white dress she wore.

Mattie said, "Leamon sho dress nice. No one knows where he gettin' dem fine clothes…."

"Sears and Roebuck and Ward catalogs," replied Julia, as she ate watermelon.

Ann added, "I ain't seed nothin' like his clothes in dem big catalog from Chicago. But you can buy everything from dem catalogs—clothes, shoes, and all things for da house."

"He go to Greenwood sometimes. I think he gets dem there." "You know, I like ta see a man dress himself nice, not wear overhalls all da time. But dress nice like white men in Greenwood do," said Mattie. "Men like women ta dress pretty, and women want men ta fix themselves up, too."

"Paul got a nice new lady, who dresses nice. I always liked Rose Davis," said Julia.

They all looked across the picnic ground at Rose, who was helping with the children's races. She was an attractive, plump, middle-aged widow who lived on a nearby plantation.

"Paul always get nice ladies," stated Mattie. They laughed.

"I have ta tell y'all da good news," said Mrs. Jessup. "Ruth been going to Greenwood, she goin' to finish eighth grade and get herself a certificate. Ruth goin' be a teacher, so she ain't gotta work da fields 'til she die."

The others at the table were surprised, smiling, and proud of Ruth. All the women suddenly looked up, and so did people all across the picnic grounds as an airplane flew overhead across the sky. The group waved to the airplane, cheering. As it flew out of sight, the picnic grounds buzzed with comments and conversations about the rare sight.

"Dis world is changing, changing so fast. We got horseless carriages, and now we got machines that fly," Mattie said.

As she ate and listened to the others talking, she realized the world was changing. Something new was coming about, and things would never be the same. But she also knew things in Money would probably never change fast enough for her. Even with all the new machines, it was no different for the Negroes that lived in Money or anywhere in the South.

The children's races were completed and the four winners ran to Paul. Little Laura, age eight, was smiling, happy, and proud of how fast she ran in the race. Paul gave each of the children a prize, which was a stick of peppermint candy, and the children raced away with joy eating their candy. Looking at the children run, Estella noticed a young man standing by a table observing her. Since she did not know him, she ignored him. Meanwhile her thoughts turned back to her Grandfather and Uncles sitting at the table with Pastor Lockwood; as usual, they were speaking their minds.

"Yes, I had a small fish market in Greenwood. I was buyin' fish from different folks. It was makin' good money, but after two years

I knew I had ta sell it, cause I was taking customers from a white man's store. I did'n' wanna wound up dead like so many other Negro folks who open a store givin' a white man competition. So, I sold it to a Mr. Jackson who was eager for my store, and six months later he was found dead hung up in a tree." Moans were heard from the men at the table.

Reverend Lockwood added, "dey don't wanna see a Negro man do nothin' worthwhile round here. Dey keep ya poor, and soon as you figure out a way to make good money, dey wanna kill ya."

"Yeah, hard ta make a good living in Mississippi, and dey make it impossible for a Negro man ta make it. I'm headed North," added Leamon.

"So, you finally gonna make da move you been talkin' bout," asked Paul.

"Gotta make it now! Can't make the kind of money I want down here. I don't care how much money I might make down here Paul 'cause it sho ain't the money a Negro man can make if 'n he go North."

"Dey want everything segregated and ta keep us po," Paul added. Reverend Lockwood put down the food he was eating. "You know, I often wonder. White folks think dey so Christian and holy, but wanna keep churches segregated. Churches fo' white folks and churches fo' Negro folks—now what's so holy bout dat?"

"I think dat will change someday; they'll make it so white and Negro folks can worship together," Mr. Jessup said.

"I wants to know when day will comes," said Paul.

"I ain't worried 'bout goin' ta church with 'em; I just wanna make money like dey do," explained Leamon.

"All da best money ain't on land. You can do good with a fishing boat, too," said the reverend.

"Who got money fo' a boat?" asked Mr. Jessup.

"Negro folks own boats down in Louisiana, making money catching fish and shrimp," Paul told them.

"If I had a boat, I'd catch lots of fish in the Mississippi River." Pastor Lockwood leaned back chuckling.

"I ain't no fisherman, I only know farming; but I sho would like to own my own land," said Mr. Jessup. "I'd grow all kinda things to make big money when I sell 'em."

"Dey was supposed to give us land when we were freed, but dey change dey mind. We sho wouldn't be down and po today like we are, if we had our own land."

"You say ya goin' up North, Leamon?"

"Yeah, I gotta go North, Reverend; gotta get far away from here….maybe Memphis"

"Memphis, Tennessee ain't far North enough, it's still da South. Gota Chicago."

"I don't know nobody in Chicago," Leamon said.

"Well, Leamon, my cousin and his wife live in Chicago. I can write dem a letter, and tell 'em you comin' to Chicago and give ya a letter to take with ya."

Leamon looked overcome with joy. "Thank ya, Reverend. I truly thank ya."

Pastor Lockwood continued, "Ya can make real money, big money like ya talk bout, in Chicago."

All this talk about going to Chicago or up North was just talk—all Estella wanted to do was go to Greenwood and get better schooling. Just like Ruth Jessup. But how could she do it? She also knew the family needed her to help work the cotton fields. Greenwood was where she wanted to be—but how?

Estella noticed her granddad walking toward her, "Papa," Estella asked, as Paul took a seat near her, "I wants to go to Greenwood."

"Why you wants to go to Greenwood, gal?" "I wants me some good schooling."

"Well, gal, if you want better schooling, I'll see you get better schoolin'!"

Estella smiled; it was the best news ever. She was so happy; she wrapped her arms around her Grandfather's neck. "Oh, Papa, you mean it? Thank you, thank you Papa!"

CHAPTER 8

Love Comes to Money

Zac Patterson was working in the cotton field in the hot sun along with a new friend Leroy Reynolds, who was helping him load cotton on a wagon that was headed to the nearby gin for processing.

"You know, this here is hard work for a boy your age!" he told Leroy.

"Who you callin' a boy?" Leroy responded, "I works as good as any man in this here field! If you don't believe me, you just try to keep up with me!"

"I don't mean nuttin' by it—don't you go gettin' mad." "I ain't mad, but you need to watch your mouth! Okay?"

"Okay. Well, where is that there sister of yours? What her name?" Zac said with a big smile.

"What you wanna know fo'?"

"I kinda like her and wants to know her better."

"Telling me you like her, Leroy said, "ain't goin' to do you no good—you best be tellin' her!"

Zac wasn't sure what to say next, knowing he wanted to get on the kid's best side.

"Here come my sister now," Leroy said, pointing to his left. Zac looked up to see the tall dark girl he had seen a few times before on the way to church. When the wagon came to a stop in front of the small white church, Paul jumped down and offered a helping hand to Julia and his granddaughter. He noticed Reverend Lookwood's wagon, and another that belonged to the Rice family. Mr. Rice was standing close by, dressed in his Sunday blue suit. His wife, holding his arm, wore a bright yellow dress with red flowers.

As they all walked up the steps into church, Estella was thinking more about the Sunday dinner with Zac than the Reverend Lockwood's sermon. She always liked to hear the music and the choir singing, but today it seemed like the sermon and the choir carried on much too long.

As usual, as everyone filed out of the church; the women stood in one group outside on the lawn and the men in another group. Estella stood by, watching and wishing they could get back home soon. She looked over at her mother coming toward her.

"You ready to go, gal," her mother asked. "Yes, Mama, I sho am!"

"Well, you know how your granddad gets, when he talkin' to the reverend."

Estella looked over at the group of men, saying, "I'm going to walk home—I'll see y'all when you get home. I can finish cooking the corn and chicken."

Julia laughed, as she saw her daughter walking down the road toward their house. She knew the girl was excited to see Zac.

It took about a half-hour to walk home; although it was hot, she didn't mind the walk. She entered the kitchen and pumped some cool water into a big bowl, washing the dust and sweat from her face and hands. She took down her mother's apron from the hook next to the sink. Since most of the food had been cooked the day before, all she had to do was fry the chicken and cook the corn.

As she finished shucking the corn, she heard wagons outside the house. Looking outside the kitchen window, she saw her family's wagon and the reverend's. Just a few minutes later, Zac's wagon pulled into the yard.

"I got the table all set," she told her mother.

"That's good! I think everyone hungry. Time to set down, y'all, and say grace," Julia told the group.

Estella looked at Zac, happy to see him looking at her too. She motioned for him to sit across the table from her. For the next hour, everyone enjoyed the good meal. Estella enjoyed laughing and having a good meal with her family. She wished it could always be peaceful and fun like this in the South.

CHAPTER 9

The Movie

All day Estella could not stop thinking about going to the movies with Zac. She wished she had a pretty new dress to wear, and new shoes, but she didn't.

"Gal, come here," her mother called out from a bedroom at the back of the house. "I got something for you." Walking into her mother's bedroom, Estella could not believe her eyes—her mother was holding a blue dress she had made. A big smile crossed her face; *where did her mother get this dress from? She wondered.* As if to read her mind, her mother added," I made it for your birthday, but I know you need it now." She smiled at her daughter.

"I love you, Mama," Estella whispered, as she hugged her mother. Taking the dress, Estella hurried from the room so she could try it on. Once in her room, she quickly tried on the beautiful new blue dress. She could feel the soft material. She still could not believe she had a new dress and was going to the movie with Zac. This was the best of days.

Zac was coming around ten o'clock, and she was busy getting ready, taking a bath, fixing her hair and washing her old worn shoes.

She used lard to make them shine. It was now twenty past ten, and Zac was not be found.

"What you walking up and down the floor for, gal," her mother asked. "That boy will get here when he gets here. What you know about him, anyway?"

"He's fun to be around—and he is nice, too," Estella answered. "He likes me and I like him!"

Julia smiled and said, "When a gal get your age, she starts thinkin' about boys. Remember what I told you 'bout boys, and don't you be bringin' no baby back here!"

"Oh Mama, I ain't goin' to bring no baby home!" Estella smiled and gave her mother a big hug.

At last Zac was crossing the front yard. She knew it because the dogs were barking. "Sorry I'm late—my pa ain't feeling good and I had to fix him some dinner fo' I left." Zac explained.

"Come on in," Estella motioned to the boy, "and have a seat, I'll be ready in a little while."

"Gal, if you ain't ready now, you ain't never gonna be ready," her mother said, laughing.

Estella's Grandfather, Paul, walked slowly over to Zac and asked, "What time y'all goin' to get back here, boy?"

"Soon as the show let out and I can get that old wagon down the road back here, Mr. Reynolds."

"Leave that boy alone," Julia told Paul.

"I just want this boy to know I don't want him to take a long time gettin' that gal back home."

Estella was finally all dressed and ready to go to the movie; as she walked into the room, she knew her family and Zac were admiring her new blue dress. Her mother smiled, saying, "You lookin' like you goin' somewhere."

"I'm ready," Estella added. Zac, with a big smile, took her hand and guided her toward the front door. They continued to hold hands across the front yard as Zac stepped up into the wagon and leaned down to help her take a place next to him. Taking the reins, he slapped them against the mule's backside and down the bumpy dirt road they went—toward Greenwood.

Estella turned to look over at Zac, noticing he was looking at her and not the road ahead. "You need to be watchin' where this mule is taking us!" she laughed, pointing toward the road ahead.

"This here mule gonna stay in the road, without me lookin' at him all the time."

"You better look anyway, boy." She looked deep into Zac's eyes for the first time, and her heart skipped a beat. Zac put his arm around her shoulder, pulling her closer to him.

"You one good-lookin' gal, and you a hard worker, too!" Estella could feel Zac's hand rubbing her arm, and she started to feel things she had never felt before.

This was the second time she had been to a movie house. The first time, her Grandfather had taken her. Sharecroppers had little money for such things—after all, the movie cost six cents, and that was a lot of money for her family and many other families in her little town. But Zac was going to pay her way.

"What the movie goin' to be about Zac?"

"About a bad man in Chicago, my friend Fred done told me about it. He said it was a good movie, lots of people gettin' shot!"

Estella did not think she would like to see people getting killed. But the only movie she had ever seen before was fun. Maybe this movie would be just as good.

54

The wagon finally rolled into the small town of Greenwood. To Estella, it was the biggest town she knew of because she had never been beyond Greenwood. It was so exciting to her to see so many cars, houses, stores, parks, and people. Her town of Money was tiny compared to Greenwood.

When they approached the center of town and the movie house, a Model-T Ford passed by their wagon. The driver of the noisy car blew his horn at them. His horn made a "woga woga" sound as he passed. Within minutes, they reached the brown and yellow movie house with its large marquee that hung from the roof. Estella looked up to read the words "SCAR FACE"—starring Paul Muni.

"We here," Zac said as he pulled back on the reins to make the old mule stop the wagon. Zac climbed down from the wagon seat, walked over to where Estella was sitting, reached for her hand, and helped her down. "Wait here, gal. I'll get the tickets."

Standing in front of the movie house, Estella noticed some white children at the ticket window buying tickets too. Then she looked over to the window where Zac was standing. Over his head a sign read "COLORED ONLY," making it clear that Negroes were not equal to whites.

Returning to her side, Zac pointed to a door marked "COLORED ONLY." "We got to go upstairs to where our seats be."

Opening the door and climbing to the top of the stairs, they moved down the aisle past several other moviegoers until they found the last two seats near the front of the balcony. "We got good seats," Zac whispered to her, as the big screen in the front of them came to life with sound and picture.

The announcer was talking about a man named Hitler coming to power. The screen showed men in uniform jumping out of trucks and hitting people as they ran down the street. "And in Italy, Hitler has a friend in Mussolini," the announcer went on, talking about Hitler, Mussolini, Germany, and Italy. These were people and places neither she nor Zac had heard of, and they didn't know why the people were being beaten and chased. Next the announcer was talking about a place called Japan—again more attacks on the screen showed men in uniforms, this time with guns shooting at houses that had smoke coming from them. It was all so confusing and exciting at the same time for both of them.

"Now in the movies" the announcer continued, "*Gone with the Wind* will be one of the best movies of the year."

Within just a few minutes, she thought she had saw and learned more looking at this movie than she ever would in her little school books. When the newsreel was over, the movie started. She felt Zac's arm wrap around her shoulder, pulling her toward him. She started to feel warm all over. This was a new feeling, one that she liked and disliked at the same time.

The movie was about Al Capone. He looked mean and was short and she noticed a long scar on one side of his face. Now she realized why the movie was called "Scarface."

"Is that why they call this here movie *Scarface*," she asked Zac loudly.

"Shhhh, gal." Zac whispered, putting his finger to his lips. "They goin' to put us out of here if 'n you talk that loud."

Zac had his hand on her leg, and that warm feeling was getting even hotter. She was trying to keep her eyes on the movie, but it was getting harder because of Zac's hands—one around her arm and the other on her leg. That was getting more of her attention than the movie at this point. Looking toward the movie screen, she saw a man shooting a gun that seemed to shoot lots of bullets from a moving car window.

"I never saw a gun shoot like that," she told Zac. Once again Zac placed his finger to his lips. "Shhhhhhh, gal—they goin' to put us out of here!"

Just then a light filled the room from behind them and a little fat, bald white man came down the aisle toward them. He pointed his finger at them and motioned for them to come with him. "Why you niggers talkin' loud? People can't hear the movie!" he told them.

Not knowing what to say, Zac responded, "Sorry, sir!"

"Make sure I don't have to come up here again, 'cause next time I'll throw you both out of here!" Ya hear me, boy?"

"Yes, sir, we be real quiet," Zac promised the man.

"Make sure y'all do!" And with that, he turned, walking back into the dark movie house.

"I told you, gal, don't talk so loud—they was gonna put us out!" he scolded.

She felt bad about almost being thrown out of the move. Back in their seats, the man on the screen was loading boxes onto trucks inside a garage when some other men walked into the garage and started shooting again, this time killing the men loading the trucks. She winced at the scene on the big screen and then felt Zac putting his arm around her again, but this time he leaned in as she turned toward him. He kissed her on her lips very softly, making her heart beat fast. She had never been kissed by anyone outside of her family, and never on the lips—it felt totally new to her, but she knew she liked the feeling. The movie played on and on, she quickly lost track of what was happening on the big screen. She could only think of Zac and all the new feelings she was having.

On the way home, they talked about the movie. "Chicago must be a whole lot bigger than Greenwood," Zac told her.

"You think I will ever find a way to go to a place like that?" "I reckon so—when you are a little older," he said.

Looking up the road, she saw the same man, with bib overalls and straw hat that she had seen on the way into town. But this time he was on the other side of the road in front of the gray house, painting a fence. Just as they passed by, she asked, "Ain't that the same man we saw on the way into town?"

"Sho is—he is working hard in this here hot sun!"

She knew it was even hotter now than it was earlier; the sun had been out all day, and it was like fire. And as they continued back to Money, the heat was almost unbearable for both of them; sweat ran down their faces.

"It must be over ninety degrees," Zac said, "look in the back of the wagon; I keep two sun hats under the seat." Placing the big straw hats on their heads, the sun was now blocked from their bodies, and they felt much cooler. The heat was not the only thing they had to deal with—the bugs were biting and buzzing, making their ride even more miserable. *This was no time to sit close to each other and kiss and hug. The slow hot ride home seemed to take forever, Estella thought.* At last they neared Wildwood Plantation.

"We almost there," Zac sighed. "Ain't too fast for me!"

The familiar bend in the road always meant that she was either leaving or entering Wildwood Plantation. Now at last the wagon pulled into her front yard; Zac climbed down from the wagon and helped her down from her very uncomfortable seat. Zac looked into her eyes and asked, "Well, gal, did you like the movie? Was it fun?"

"I had a good time, a real good time!" she answered, looking back in to his eyes.

"We best be goin' in the house and get out this hot sun!"

The two walked into the small house, finding her mother and brother sitting at the table drinking lemonade, with a big tub of ice next to the table. After their long, very hot ride from Greenwood, a cold drink was just what they needed.

Her Grandfather Paul sat in the big brown chair in the corner of the room, fast asleep, snoring loudly. "Y'all have a good time," her mother added.

"We done had a real good time, Mama!"

"That there lemonade is looking mighty good, Mrs. Reynolds! It's good, when you settin' in the sun on that hot wagon seat."

"Leroy—give them a cup so they can have some lemonade," Julia said, pointing at the jar of lemonade sitting in the center of the table.

Drinking down the cold liquid, Estella could feel her body cooling off right away. Zac took a rag from his pocket, walked over to the tub where the ice sat, and dipped the rag into the cold water. Wringing the water out, he placed the cold rag to his forehead. "Now that feels good!" he mumbled.

Looking over at her Grandfather, Estella noticed that he was sweating too. "We better wake Papa and give him some of this lemonade, before he gets too hot from all this heat!"

Zac drank two cups of the lemonade, while he and the family talked about the movie they had seen. He noticed the sun was beginning to set through a window nearby, "Guess I best be going 'fo it gets too late and too dark."

Estella rose to look out the window too. "I'll walk you out to the wagon."

"Thanks for bringing Estella home on time," Julia told the boy. Zac opened the door for Estella and they walked to the old wooden wagon, where his mule stood drinking water and eating corn.

"I had a real good time," Estella said

"Yes, me too—thanks for the lemonade." Zac turned and kissed her fully on her lips, and quickly jumped into the wagon seat and picked up the reins.

"I'll see you in the fields." Before she could answer, the wagon started to move down the dirt road toward the sunset.

The day after her big trip to the movies with Zac, Estella could not stop thinking about how much she had enjoyed the whole day— the ride to Greenwood, the news about other faraway places she had never heard of, the cars, the people, the houses in Greenwood…and most of all, Zac and the way he made her feel when he touched her or sat close to her. The feeling of being near a boy other than her family was new to her.

"Gal, what you doin'?" her mother called to her. "It's time to go to the field!" Her words broke Estella's train of thought and she turned from the joy of the trip to the long hot day of work in the cotton field. The only good thing about going to the field was that she would see Zac, and that made the day worth looking forward to. A week after her trip to Greenwood with Zac, Estella was still thinking about what a good time she had. Zac asked if she wanted to go to another movie with him, to see a Western. She could not believe he was going to take her to the movies again so soon.

"I sho do!"

Zac looked at her and smiled, and her heart skipped a beat.

Estella said yes to the movie before she asked her mother, and she hoped it would be okay.

"Mama, Zac wants to take me to the movies again, next week. Is that gonna be all right with you?"

"Why that boy keep taking you to the movies?"

"I don't know—he just like being with me, and I like being with him!"

"Don't you go gettin' too sweet on that boy! It's okay this time, but you got to wait a time after that, before you get carried away with that boy," she warned.

Paul was in the next room and had overhead their conversation about Estella and Zac going to the movies. He called from behind the door, "Gal, you best listen to your mama and don't go head over heels for that boy!"

CHAPTER 10

Leamon Goes North

Leamon sometimes helped Mrs. Carson around the house and yard to make a little extra money. One day he was helping to unload a wagon full of wood, when Mrs. Carson asked if he wanted something cold to drink.

"That would be right kind of you, ma'am."

"You should come in the house and take a little break—it's hot out here and you are sweating hard. Mr. Carson and Chip have gone to Greenwood." Leamon reluctantly followed her into the big white house and stood near the front door.

Mrs. Carson was a tall red-headed woman with green eyes and very pale skin. She always dressed nicely and was friendly with everyone, even the Negro people she met. Leamon noticed she looked at him a little funny and always stood near him, when her husband was not around. At first he didn't think much of it, but now standing in the house all alone with her, Leamon became very nervous. This could get him hung, he was thinking.

"I don't know if I oughta be here alone in this here house with you, ma'am."

"Who's gonna know, boy, but you and me? Why are you shaking, boy?"

Moving closer and closer to Leamon, she said, "You are one good-looking strong Negro boy. You ever been with a white woman and had your way with her?"

Leamon's heart was beating so fast, he could hear it beating. "I think I need to get back to work, ma'am."

The woman stepped closer, whispering in his ear. "I think you need to show me a good time—and if you don't, I will tell Mr. Benson you tried to kiss me, and you know what he will do to you!" Taking Leamon by the arm, she walked toward the bedroom at the back of the house.

Just before they reached the door to the room, she turned and looked into Leamon's eyes, and for the first time in his life, he looked into a white woman's face and eyes. He knew he could be hung for thinking about a white woman, but being so close to her and her bedroom, he knew if other white folks found out, he would be hung. Suddenly he jumped, and so did Mrs. Carson. They heard a door close—had Mr. Carson and Chip come home? Turning toward the front of the house, they saw the local mailman, holding a package and looking intently at them.

"I got a package for you, Mrs. Carson," the mailman said with a scowl, handing her a small brown box. The mailman turned toward the rear steps and gave them one last mean look, as he walked down the steps and onto the small path leading back onto the road.

"I best be leaving here, ma'am—if 'n that mailman saw you standing up so close to me like that, the Klan may come after me!" Leamon could hardly get the words out.

"I think that's a good idea—Leamon," Mrs. Carson replied. Leamon couldn't wait to say goodbye, and almost ran from the

Carson's house to his sister Julia's house on the other side of the railroad tracks. Nearly out of breath from running so fast, Leamon found Estella alone; as she turned, she immediately knew something was wrong.

"What's wrong?" Estella asked.

"Gal, stop asking questions, and come on with me so you can help me get my things together."

"Where you goin', Leamon?" "You don't need to know that!"

Estella followed Leamon, who was almost running out of the house and into the nearby woods. "I need you to go to my house and pack up me some clothes and make some sandwiches—peanut butter and jelly, and some ham too. Grab me some pecans, maybe an apple, and some cheese. Oh, and don't forget socks and two towels. Now, get goin', gal!"

Leamon added, "And if anybody ask you, have you seen me…tell them no. Now get goin'. I'll stay here 'til you get back."

Estella ran toward Leamon's house, not knowing what going was on. Why was her Uncle talking about leaving Money? Why did he need all the things he told her to bring him? Once at her Uncle's house, she went into the small kitchen to get the food Leamon had asked for. She found the towels and socks out in the back of the house on the clothes line. Wrapping everything in a big towel, she started back to meet her Uncle in the woods.

Walking down the road just in front of the woods where her Uncle was hiding, she saw four men on horseback coming toward her. Knowing if they saw her it would not be good, she ran into the nearby woods and watched them go by. She recognized two of the men—the man riding a dark brown horse was Mr. Carson, and the other was Chip, his son, who was riding a small black and white pony. As they grew closer, she also saw Mr. Hillman, the mailman in town and Sheriff Jones.

"When I catch up to that nigger, I'm gonna string him up to the biggest tree I can find. That nigger, tryin' to rape my wife—I'll show him to keep his hands off a white woman! You just wait!"

She hoped they were not talking about her Uncle, but deep inside, she knew they were. Now it all made sense. Just as the men on horseback passed Estella's hiding place, the man on the lead horse put his hand into the air, and they all stopped.

"I hear something," Sheriff Jones whispered.

Her heart stopped; she knew what might happen if they found her. And she was afraid of what they would do to her Uncle if they found him. The men climbed down from their horses and moved slowly into the woods, coming closer and closer to where she was hiding. She could see Chip's dirty boots just above her head. She had covered herself with leaves, hoping that they would keep her from being seen.

Just as Chip turned in her direction, Mr. Carson called out, "It's just a deer—I saw him over yonder!"

Just then, Estella felt something crawling down her leg and looked down to see a big brown spider. She wanted to scream. She knew that if she moved too much, she would be seen, so she let the spider crawl slowly down her leg. She hoped it would go faster, as fear ran up her spine and sweat ran down her face. She peeked from under the dry leaves and found that the men were getting back on their horses, and she watched them ride off down the small dirt road, leaving little puffs of dust behind them.

Moving slowly to uncover herself from the leaves, she walked deeper into the woods to where her Uncle was hiding, hoping to find him. She ran as fast as she could to the place she had left her Uncle. "Hey, gal," Leamon called out to his niece. "Did you get all the stuff I told you to get?"

"Yes, Uncle, but why are you running and hiding out in this here woods?"

"You don't need to know that."

"But I saw some men on horses a little ways back," she said. "I know them—Mr. Carson, Chip, and the mailman."

"Did they see you, gal?"

"No. I was hiding in a low spot."

"You always been one smart gal—but I gotta go." "Where you going?"

"I told you, stop asking questions, gal; sometimes it's just best you don't know. Now you need to get on your way home."

"What do I say if Mama or Grandpa ask if I seed you?"

"Just tell them no—I guess in time y'all will find out where I went. Now you better get out of here, gal—I'll be just fine," Leamon smiled and gave his niece a big hug. "Now get out of here—go on now!"

Estella turned and walked slowly through the woods toward home. She could only think about her Uncle, and hoped he was not in too much trouble. Just as she reached the road near her house, she noticed some men on horses in the front yard talking to her grandfather and mother. Not wanting to be seen, Estella moved into some tall bushes near the side of the road. She was close enough to hear what was being said, but far enough away not to be seen. She knew the men, because they were the same men she had seen in the woods

— Mr. Carson, Chip, and the mailman. Mr. Carson was asking her mother if she had seen Leamon. Her mother told him she hadn't seen Leamon since yesterday.

"Tell that boy the law is lookin' for him—and he better hope the Sheriff finds him before I do!"

"What's he done?" her mother asked. "You just tell him what I said."

Before her mother could say another word, the three men on their horses rode off down the dusty road. Estella watched from her hiding place. She waited until the men disappeared before she moved from her hiding place and began walking toward her front yard, where her mother and Grandfather stood.

"Hey gal, where you been?"

"I went over to Leamon's house, but he ain't home."

Her Grandfather looked at her with a funny expression. "You didn't see him, gal?"

"No, Papa—he musta been out working somewhere."

"Some men come looking for him," her mother told her. "I don't know what goin' on with Leamon, but the men said he was in a heap of trouble—for what, he don't tell us." Julia looked at her daughter and asked again, "You sho you ain't seed Leamon, gal?"

"No, I ain't seed him."

"Well, the bugs are starting to bite; we best get into the house," warned her Grandfather.

Leamon knew just how he was going to get up North. Every day the train came down the tracks from Greenwood and dropped off an empty box car at the cotton gin, to be loaded with cotton bales, going up North. Leamon knew that before the end of the day, another train would hook up to the full boxcar and take it North. Waiting in the woods until just about daybreak, he found the old wooden box-car, sitting just where he knew it would be.

Leamon hoped the boxcar would be unlocked so he could hide behind the bales. To his surprise, he was able to push the doors open and climb inside. He found the bales of cotton just a little ways behind the door, giving him just enough room to get inside. Inside the dirty boxcar he found a small space between the bales—it was the perfect spot. If anyone looked into the boxcar, they would not see him.

As he crawled between the tall bales, dust and flakes of cotton fell on him; quietly he squeezed in and sat back, waiting for the train to move. It was quiet and dark, and soon he fell asleep. It wasn't long before a big hard bump woke him up, and he could feel the train moving forward. He was scared, but glad to know he was on his way to a new life up North.

Julia knew that no one had seen her brother for more than two days. Something was wrong. It was not like him to not come by and let her know if he was going somewhere. She also knew that sometimes when a Negro man disappeared—something bad had happened to him.

Paul looked at his granddaughter over the dinner table that night and asked about the men on horses that had stopped at the house. "Ain't nobody seen hide or hair of your Uncle for more than two days. What you know about where he is, gal? And don't lie to me!"

"He told me not to tell nobody," Estella said looking at her mother.

Her mother waited for the next words her daughter would say; she knew the girl must know where Leamon was. "Come on, gal, spit it out!"

"Okay, Mama. Yes, I come home and Leamon was here—he told me to fix him a few things because he had to get out of here fast. I got everything he told me to get and met him in the woods out yonder."

"Why he got to go so fast, gal?"

"I don't know—something musta happened at the Carson's place, 'cause'n that's where he was befo' he come here."

Her mother listened as Paul and Estella talked about Leamon. She knew her brother would be all right, because he knew the woods, the land, the town, the people, and how to live off the land.

"I hope Mr. Carson don't find him. He is hoppin' mad—no tellin' what he might do. I think my brother goin' to be all right. I just know he will," Julia added.

The days and weeks went by, and at last a letter came from Chicago. It was a letter from Leamon saying he was doin' all right and making a little money picking up coal along the railroad tracks. He would save the small coal pieces in bushel baskets until they were full enough to sell to people to heat their houses. Since the coal was free and going to waste anyway, it was a good way to make money.

The whole family was overjoyed—the news spread fast. They all knew, including Mattie and Leroy, about the letter. They talked about how it must be to live in a big city like Chicago.

Paul told Leroy, "It must be nice to just pick up coal and not cotton to make good money that you can just keep." Estella knew Chicago had to be better than Greenwood or Money.

CHAPTER **11**

A Better School

I t had been a long hot summer. Estella had been looking forward to going to the big school for Negroes. She had been packing all summer, long before she needed to. The days went by so slowly, but at last there were only two days left until she would be off to Greenwood and the big school. The night before she was to leave, she could not sleep. She would wake up often, and at last, it was six o'clock in the morning, daylight streaming through her bedroom window—time to get out of bed. Finally, the day she had been waiting for so long had arrived, she was going to Greenwood to the big schoolhouse.

She knew it was going to be the best thing for her to stay in Greenwood all week and come home some weekends. Her Grandfather Paul made her brother Leroy take her the almost eleven miles from Money to Greenwood in the family's old wooden wagon, pulled by the mule they called Joe.

"It hard to make Joe go and he always go slow," Leroy said shaking his head.

Estella chimed in, "The wagon and the mule is better than walking!"

On the way to Greenwood, Leroy teased his sister about trying to get smarter than him, and how he would always be bigger and know more than her. "How you know you always gonna know mo' than me?" she asked her brother, in her typical sassy way. Leroy didn't answer; he just shook his head.

As the wagon moved closer to their destination, she could not stop thinking about how great it would be to be in a big town, a big school with a new teacher and new friends. She also knew she would have better books—and best of all, she would learn more.

"Can't you make this thing go any faster, boy?"

"No, this here wagon ain't goin to move no faster 'cause'n you want it to! We goin' to get there when we get there!"

And sure enough, just like he had promised, she could finally see some of the houses and buildings that lined the edge of the small city of Greenwood.

"We here, gal!"

Estella was so excited—she had been in Greenwood before, but this time was different. She would live in town all week, go to a new school, have new teachers, and for the first time in her life be on her own. Before she knew it, the wagon was in front of the bright red two-story school. It was the most beautiful building she had ever seen, and it was her new school.

"Hey, gal—what you waiting fo'? Get down so I can help you with your things."

Jumping down from the wagon seat, she noticed a short Negro woman with her hair pulled neatly into a bun, wearing a bright blue dress and glasses, walking toward her.

"Hello. My name is Mrs. Williams, and I am the headmistress here at Greenwood School. You must be the new girl."

Estella was shocked to find a woman being her school's headmistress. "Yes ma'am, I guess so."

"You guess so? You don't know," the woman asked her.

Estella just looked down at her feet, at her almost worn-out shoes that were getting too small. Mrs. Williams noticed, "Look up, hold your head high, girl. Always hold your head high and let people see how proud you are of being who you are!"

Looking up into the woman's eyes, Estella saw for the first time in her life a strong Negro woman who didn't run from anything.

"Young man, take this girl's bags from the back of wagon and carry them to the front door of the school. Estella, you will be living with Ruth Jessup?"

"Yes ma'am. She live in Greenwood with her Aunt and Uncle."

"Yes, Ruth lives just down the road from the school," Mrs. Williams added.

Estella looked around as she walked into the school beside Mrs. Williams. The school was so big, with classrooms...a lot of them, unlike her small one-room church school back in Money. Leroy also liked what he saw; it was the best school he had ever seen.

"You best be gettin' on the way back to Money," she told her brother.

"Let him stay and look over the school. I want to show both of you our school. Since it is Saturday, there are no classes, but some of our students are here so they can get more schoolin' in their free time."

The two children followed Mrs. Williams down the first floor hallway, stopping as they walked while she told them about the classes and teachers in each room. Estella thought it was her dream come true; this was the best day of her life. At the end of the hallway was a small wooden staircase, leading to the classrooms on the second floor.

"Let's go upstairs to the lunch room."

As they climbed the staircase, and entered the lunch room, Estella glanced around, realizing that the room was as big as her whole school back home. There were several tables on one side of the room and a small stage on the other end.

"This sho is a nice place, Mrs. Williams," Leroy said.

"I'm glad you like it."

Walking back down the staircase, she led them to her small office, near the front entrance of the school. "Have a seat, children," she said, pointing to the two wooden chairs in front of her desk. "I am glad you like our school. Ruth Jessup told me a lot about you, Estella." Not knowing what to say, the girl just smiled. "Young man, I need to talk to your sister alone, if you don't mind."

"No, ma'am. I needs to be gettin' back home, befo' it gets dark." "Well then, be careful, young man, and please close the door behind you." Glancing over at Estella, Mrs. Williams asked, "so, child, do you like our school?"

"Oh yes, Mrs. Williams! This must be the best school in the whole world!"

Mrs. Williams smiled. "Well, young lady, there are many schools bigger and ones that have many more students, but I like to think none of them are better. Now tell me about your school in Money." "Well, we learned to read and count, and sometimes my teacher talk about how to cook and sew. But I can count and read a little bit too."

"Did you learn anything about history or geography?" "No, but I can add and do some take-away."

"Take-away is called subtraction. Did your teacher in Money tell you that?"

"No ma'am—she called it take-away."

"Well, now, Greenwood Grade School is here to help you to become a smart young lady and to learn more about the world we live in."

Estella did not understand exactly everything Mrs. Williams was saying, but she knew a bigger and better school had to be good for her.

"Just how will you eat during the week, Estella?"

"My brother will bring me food from home, and when I go home, I am goin to bring something to eat back with me."

"That's good. I know you will be living with the Jessups, just down the road."

"Yes ma'am. Ruth and her Uncle Carl goin' to come pick me up here in a little while."

Estella and Mrs. Williams walked to the school entrance and waited for Ruth and her Uncle to come. Within minutes, Estella noticed a familiar wagon coming toward them.

"Hi, Estella," Ruth said, waving from the wagon seat. Her Uncle pulled back to stop the mule in front of the school. Ruth jumped down to give Estella a big hug. "I'm so glad to see you!"

Ruth looked over at Mrs. Williams, who peered over her glasses at them, saying, "I'm glad to see you both." Ruth and Estella talked for a few minutes; Ruth was excited to tell Estella about the new school.

"Well, ladies, it's almost dinner time, I guess we best be gettin' on," Carl Jessup said.

"Goodbye, Mrs. Williams," Mr. Jessup said, as he walked out the door to his wagon, climbing in and motioning to Ruth and Estella to join him.

"Goodbye, girls!" Mrs. Williams said, waving to them, as the wagon moved slowly down the road toward the Jessup house on the other side of the railroad tracks. Pulling up to the house, they could see Ann Jessup standing in the door of her small two-edroom box-shaped wooden house. She welcomed Ruth, Estella, and her husband, as they climbed down from their wagon.

"Auntie, this be Estella, the gal I told you about—she's goin to school in Greenwood with me. Her mama and granddad are good friends of my mama and daddy."

"Glad to meet you. Come on in, I got dinner ready," Ann said, giving them a big hug.

As they walked into the house, Estella could smell the familiar aroma of fried chicken and spices filling the house. Looking around the inside of the Jessup house, she saw a small living room that had a big pot-belly stove in the center with a table to one side, and on the table were mashed potatoes, fried chicken, sweet potato pie, and corn on the cob.

"I know y'all must be hungry," Ann said, pointing to the table full of food.

"You right about that," said Carl, as he was washing his hands at the kitchen sink. Motioning Ruth and Estella toward the sink, he said, "Clean hands and good food—you can't beat that!"

Taking a chair from the small wooden table he had built himself just two years ago, Mr. Jessup was eager to taste Ann's good cookin'. Ruth and Estella were still talking and washing their hands.

"Y'all better get to this table before Carl eat up all this here food from you!" Ann called out.

"Can Estella say grace," Ruth asked.

"Now Ruth, you know that's my job, but since you asked me and Estella look like a nice gal, it's okay this time." Everyone at the table lowered their heads and placed their hands together under their chins, while they waited for her to say grace.

"God bless this food, God bless my family and bless the Jessup family, and God, thank you for letting me go to the school in Greenwood."

Ann looked up, saying, "That was a nice prayer, girl." "Thank you, Mrs. Jessup."

"Let's eat, y'all, before this food get cold. Ruth, would you please pass the corn?"

The family enjoyed the dinner that Ann had prepared. Mr. Jessup asked, "Estella, how are things over in Money?"

"I guess they okay."

"How your folks," Ann asked.

"They all okay; working hard in the fields every day."

"How you like Greenwood, Estella?" "I like it a lot, ma'am."

"What's so special about Greenwood?"

"It's got a better school and better books. Ruth likes the school here in Greenwood too—she tells me it is better than that little schoolhouse back in Money."

"Well I'm glad you both can go to school here."

"And that we can put you up at our house," Carl chimed in.

Everyone at the table ate until they were as full as could be. Carl laid back in his chair, rubbing his stomach with his hand. "If I eat any more, my belly goin' to pop!"

After dinner they all moved to the front room near the big black pot-belly stove, because the night air was getting a little cool. The smell of wood burning filled the little house.

"Have you seen my brother, Estella?" Carl asked.

"I seed him at church last Sunday, and he looked okay to me." "Well, gal, do you have enough clothes with you?"

"Yes ma'am; I got a whole big old box full of clothes and some food Mama canned. My brother Leroy will be bringin' me some food from time to time so I don't eat up all your food."

"We got enough food for you and Ruth, but it's nice that your family will be helping out."

They continued to talk about church and school for nearly an hour. Then Ann told Ruth and Estella, "It's gettin' late, and you know y'all got school tomorrow."

Ruth and Estella walked back to the small bedroom near the back of the house. The two young girls talked while preparing for bed. "I can't wait for tomorrow to come, so I can go to my new school."

"Yes, I was just like you when I moved from Money to stay with my Uncle and Aunt! The school in this town is a lot better than the one-room schoolhouse in Money," Ruth said.

The next morning the sun flooded Estella's bedroom; waking both her and Ruth. "Good morning, Estella." She noticed the girl had a big smile on her face.

Estella quickly jumped from her bed. "I got to wash up and get ready for school."

"It ain't time for school yet! We got lots of time to get ready. My aunt get up befo' sun-up so she can make breakfast for my Uncle before he go to work over at the Gray's house. He's the handyman and he fixes things, cuts grass, paints, and runs errands for the Grays."

"You gals need to get in here early so I can talk to y'all before it's time for y'all to go to school," Ann called back to them.

"We better get ready now, Estella."

The two girls quickly dressed for school and headed to the kitchen, sitting close to the big black pot-belly stove, warming their hands to take away the slight chill in the house.

"You gals have a chair—I cooked up some bacon and eggs for your breakfast," Ann told them. "Ruth, did you tell Estella that she's goin' to have to help fix her food for lunch from now on and help out around the house?"

"No, but I was goin' to tell her befo' we go to school."

After breakfast they thanked Ann for their breakfast and grabbed their sweaters. Leaving the house, Estella was so excited walking to school. Her new school in Greenwood was so big, and the one back home was so small. Even the part of town where Negroes lived looked better than back home. In Greenwood, the Negro homes were not much bigger, but they were painted better and kept up bet- ter. To Estella, everything here was bigger and better. Ruth noticed Estella was not talking to her, and seemed in another world.

"Estella, what you looking at?"

"Sorry, Ruth. I was looking at how everything here—the houses, the cars, the people—all look better than back home."

"Yes, I know. I felt the same way when I first come to Greenwood."

The two girls talked and walked all the way to the schoolhouse, across the railroad tracks.

"We here finally!" Estella didn't answer right away; she just stood looking at her big beautiful new schoolhouse, and she knew her life would never be the same.

The schoolyard was full of children running, jumping, talking, and playing. Estella had never seen so many children attending school before. Her thoughts were interrupted by the school bell. "We got here just in time," Ruth told her.

Estella started to run toward the school entrance, shouting back to Ruth, "I ain't gonna be late on my first day of my new school!"

Ruth just laughed, calling out, "We still got time fo' the next bell rings in fifteen minutes."

"That's good, 'cause I don't want to be late!"

"Estella—come over here. I want you to meet some of my friends." Pulling at Estella and walking toward a small group of children talking near the edge of the school yard, Ruth called out, "Hey y'all, this here is my friend from Money. Her name is Estella."

"Nice to meet y'all," Estella said, nodding.

Ruth pointed toward the four children in front of them. "This here is Betsy, Tom, Jerry, and Mary. They my good friends and you need to know them, Estella." The six children talked briefly, until the second bell rang out. Estella saw Mrs. Williams coming toward them in the hallway.

"I hope our school will help you get up to your grade level. I will do everything I can to help you, Estella."

Estella looked at Mrs. Williams and she knew she was in good hands. "I want you to take classes in reading, math, history, and English. And I am going to give you one of our best teachers, Miss Smith. She will help you come up a grade level." Estella didn't know what to say or think. Why was Mrs. Williams taking up with her so much? She had just got here, and hadn't had time to get to know anyone but Ruth Jessup, whom she knew from Greenwood.

Walking down the long hallway, Mrs. Williams motioned back, "Come on, Estella, let's go meet Miss Smith." The two stopped at the classroom at the end of the hall; Mrs. Williams knocked on the door and a tall Negro woman opened the door. "This is Miss Smith, Estella; she will be your teacher for the next eight weeks. She will help you get up to another grade level."

"Yes, Mrs. Williams, I believe we can do just that," Estella's new teacher assured her.

"Well then, I am going to leave you two alone—that noise I hear down the hallway is disturbing the other classrooms," Mrs. Williams added, rushing down the hallway.

Standing in front of Miss Smith, Estella's head was racing; she was the second Negro woman she had met in Greenwood who looked strong and very smart.

"Well, young lady, we got lots of work to do so we can show them how smart you are!"

Estella just said, "Yes, ma'am!"

"We'll start, when my other student arrives."

Just then a short young girl entered the room, wearing a dress that Estella could tell was made out of flour sacks. She knew very well the imprint repeated on the panels from the many dresses made by her mother of the same left-over flour sacks.

"This is Mary; she will be your classmate. You two young ladies will come to this room every day, one hour before school starts, so I can help you both get to where you need to be. Mary lives near your town back home, Estella. She also went to a small one-room schoolhouse, like you."

Estella was glad to know that she and Ruth were not the only ones from a small town.

"The first thing you girls must do is get your reading up to grade level. After that, we can get to work on your math. Your school in Money started your education, but you have a ways to go at the Greenwood School, before you get to the proper grade level."

To Estella, the first day of school in Greenwood was so different; so new, and most of all, so good. The school was bigger, her teachers were better, her books newer, and she would have many new classmates. It was a whole new world for this little poor girl from Money, Mississippi.

CHAPTER **12**

The Fight

For the next eight weeks, Estella worked to get her reading and writing up to the level her teacher said it should be. Today she would get her report card. She knew that her reading skills and math was below many of her classmates'. She wanted to catch up to their level, and more than anything, wanted a good report card to take home to her family—one that they would be proud of, even her brother Leroy.

Estella looked up nervously from her desk as her teacher passed out report cards to the other students. Miss Smith just smiled as she handed a card toward Estella's shaking hand. Estella slowly opened the folded card, thinking the worst; but her fear soon turned to the biggest smile that lit up the whole classroom—after all her hard work, she received two B's and two C's.

"You are one of the hardest-working students I've ever seen," Miss Smith said, patting Estella on the shoulder.

"I done good?"

"Yes, you have done very well! We have to work on your English, so you don't say things like—done did. But I am very proud of you, and you should be proud of yourself!"

"Yes ma'am, I am!" But, before Miss Smith could say another word, Estella rushed to the door. She wanted to find Ruth and tell her about the first report card from her new school and what Miss Smith had told her. Finding Ruth in the school-yard, Estella ran toward her calling out, "Look Ruth! I got good grades, two B's and two C's!"

Ruth could see how excited Estella was to show her the report card. "It look like you got some good grades here!"

Standing close by were their friends Betsy and Tom; overhearing what was said about Estella's report card, Tom asked, "Can I see your report card, Estella?"

"Sho, you can." She was so proud, she quickly handed the paper to Tom, but his response took her by surprise.

"Your grades ain't that good, gal! But for a cotton picker—they be okay."

Estella's faced turned red and her eyes were full of fire. "Why you say bad things, Tom, bout my report card and call me a cotton picker?"

"'Cause'n you and Ruth are cotton pickers!"

She didn't like Tom using those words about her and Ruth, and before she even thought about a response, she reached out and punched Tom right on his lip, which started to bleed immediately.

"Hey, gal!" Tom shouted, pushing her to the ground. Before she could stand up, he fell on top of her, hitting her face. But Estella was a little bigger and older than Tom, and it didn't take much for her to roll him over, pinning him under her. She was ready to give him another punch, when she felt someone pulling her off Tom—it was Mrs. Williams. She called out, "You two in my office—now!"

Tom jumped up, with his lip bleeding badly, his blood all over Estella's dress. As they walked toward the school, Mrs. Williams could see that Tom's eye was beginning to swell.

As they entered Mrs. Williams' office, she asked, "What is this all about?"

"Tom called me a cotton picker!"

"Tom, did you call her a cotton picker?"

Tom looked down at his shoes, covered with dust from his fight with Estella. "Yes, ma'am."

"And why did you call her that name?" "'Cause'n she is a cotton picker!"

Once again Estella started to make a fist, but before she could hit Tom again, Mrs. Williams said, "That is not right, Tom! She may have picked cotton, but that's just the way some people earn money to feed themselves and their family, or to buy things they need. Estella, what have you got to say for yourself?"

"I hit him 'cause'n he called me a name, Mrs. Williams! And 'cause'n I don't like light-skinned niggers. They always think they be better than other folks!"

Mrs. Williams gazed over her glasses at the two children with disgust. "I feel sorry for both of you. Y'all using words like cotton picker and light-skinned niggers, fighting and disrespecting each other. I don't believe what I'm seeing and hearing! What are you two saying to each other?" Leaning down, looking very stern, Mrs. Williams pointed to the two chairs across from her desk. "We as a people will never get anywhere until we stop fighting with each other...now have a seat!"

Moving around to take a seat in her chair, their teacher reminded them about slavery, how white men made babies with Negro women. She emphasized how this act created babies with much lighter skin colors, because their fathers were white. Estella had never heard any-thing like this in her life—now she knew why some Negro people were lighter. Tom also realized for the first time why his skin was much lighter than other Negroes he knew; it was also why he felt looked down on or treated differently by dark-skin Negroes.

"Now children, say you are sorry for all this fightin' and carryin' on. Stand face to face, hold your heads high—always hold your heads high! Say you are sorry."

Estella looked at Tom. "I'm sorry." But Tom was slow to respond. Mrs. Williams looked over her glasses again, saying, "Well now.... don't take all day, young man!" "I'm sorry too," he said.

"Now you two go to your classes. I will have no more of this foolishness, understand me?"

"Yes, ma'am," the two children chimed in.

As they left Mrs. Williams' office, she saw Ruth in the hallway. "Estella—what Mrs. Williams goin' to do about y'all fightin'?" "She just made us say—we sorry," Estella explained, and before she could say more about it, the school bell rang out.

"We can talk later, Ruth—got to get to my class now. See you after school."

Walking down the hall, she saw Tom coming toward, her. Fearing another fight, she looked away from Tom as he got closer.

"Hi, Estella—can we talk?" "Not now, Tom."

"Please, Estella."

"Okay, but make it fast. I ain't goin' to be late for my class." "I just wanted you to know that I'm glad we had that fight."

She wondered if Tom was crazy for being glad about a fight. "What do you mean, Tom?"

"I never knew why I was lighter than some other Negroes in Greenwood. I'm glad Mrs. Williams talked to us 'bout that. If it wasn't for us fightin', I would not know 'bout that."

84

She looked at Tom and for the first time, she did not dislike him. She knew she had been wrong about her feelings toward lighter-skinned Negroes. "You sho right, Tom—we both know better now!" Estella walked toward her classroom, turning back to say, "Sorry, I got to get to class befo' I be late Tom!"

Estella walked into Miss Smith's classroom, while she was teaching about what Negroes needed to get ahead. "You need to know math, 'cause you need to know about how to count your money, build things, even cook. You need to know English, so you can talk better, and know how to use words, how to write, and how to read. You need to know history, so you know what happened in the past. Negroes need to start down the road toward being as smart as white people, 'cause we have a long way to go!"

Before she could raise her hand with a question, the bell rang out, meaning class was over for today. In fact, the school would be closed for a five-day break. Estella met Ruth outside in the playground; the two walked and talked as they headed to the Jessup house.

"I'm glad to be on school break, Estella. I'm goin' back to Money for three days; my daddy is comin' to get me tomorrow. Maybe you can go back with us."

"That would be good, Ruth. I ain't been home but two times since I started school here in Greenwood. And I wants to see my mama and granddaddy. I miss 'em a lot!"

"I miss my folks too. That's the only bad thing about going to school here."

Walking up to the Jessup home, the girls saw Ann Jessup watering her flowers in the front yard.

"How was school, girls?" "Good," they answered together.

"I knew y'all would be hungry, so I made some peanut butter and jelly sandwiches—they on the table."

"That sounds so good, thank you," Ruth said.

Once inside Ruth handed her friend a sandwich as they both took a seat at the kitchen table, while Ruth poured two big glasses of milk.

"I hope it don't rain in the morning, since we ridin' all the way back to Money in my Daddy's open wagon. We gonna get wet to the bone if it do."

"I hope it's a sunny day and the bugs don't be bitin' us!" Estella added.

Ruth's daddy got to Greenwood early the next day. After talking with Ann and Carl for about an hour, he motioned for Ruth and Estella to get in the back of the wagon, as he took his seat in the front. Taking the reins of the mule-drawn wagon, Roscoe slapped the reins, and off they all went, down the road to Money.

On the way the girls talked about their school in Greenwood and how different it was from their school back home. Hearing them talk about their school, Roscoe added, "Y'all lucky to be going to school in Greenwood! It one of the best things for y'all. Not many of us get to go to a good school like the Greenwood school."

Time flew as the girls talked and watched the woods, houses, and now and then a few people going by. Before she knew it, Estella realized she was home—with her mother, Grandfather, and brother in the front yard. Roscoe pulled the reins back hard on the mule. "Whoa, mule!" He shouted.

"How y'all doin'?" her Grandfather called out. The wagon finally stopped and Estella quickly jumped down from the back of the wagon, nearly falling into her mother's waiting arms.

"You finally home, Estella!"

THE ROAD FROM MONEY

"Yes, Mama—I missed you so much!"

Roscoe handed the two big boxes Estella had brought home full of some clothes and school books to Leroy. "Well y'all.... we best be gettin' down the road home too." Roscoe told them. He and Ruth waved good-bye to the family as their wagon turned down the road toward home.

"I'm so glad to have you home for a few days," her mother said, kissing her on the cheek.

"I'm glad you home too! Now you can help me put up the new chicken house," Leroy added, laughing.

She was so glad to be home that she paid no attention to her brother's comment. She took her mama's arm and walked up the steps of her shack. Before the door even opened, she could smell fried catfish.

There was nothing like her Mama's good cooking. Opening the door, there on the kitchen table was a buffet of fish, corn on the cob, greens, and apple pie.

"I bet you ain't had any good cookin' like this since you been gone to Greenwood," her mother added.

"No, Mama—not like your good cookin'!"

Estella sat in her old chair at the table, while her mother piled her plate high with food.

"How you comin' with your books, Estella," her Grandfather asked.

"I'm doin' okay, I think."

"Gal, if you don't know, who do?"

"I did good in some books, but not so good in others—that's all." During dinner, she told her family all about her new Greenwood school, her teacher and classmates. "It's good to be home, Papa. I missed y'all so much!"

"I know, but I just want you to get all the schoolin' you can get, so you ain't like me—can't read good and don't know a lot of the things I need to know. The mo' you know, the better things goin' to be for you." Paul said standing with his hands on his hips.

"I think she know too much already," Leroy said, pointing to his sister, as he ran out the shack laughing, with Estella running after him.

CHAPTER **13**

The Chicken Coop

The sound of a rooster crowing woke Estella the next morning; she rolled over to feel the bright sun on her face coming through the window next to her bed. She wanted to lie in bed a little longer, but she knew there was work to be done. She also knew her mama would be up soon to fix breakfast. Before she could get dressed, she needed to wash her face and brush her teeth; opening her bedroom door, she practically ran into her mother.

"Good morning, Estella."

"Mornin', Mama." Rubbing the sleep from her eyes, Estella looked around the kitchen. "Where Papa and Leroy?"

"Your brother and granddad are out back, working on the new chicken coop. After breakfast they want you to give them a hand."

"Oh Mama, how I gonna help them?"

"I don't know, Estella, but your granddad told me to get you out there after you eat breakfast."

She wasn't too excited about helping with a chicken coop. After eating her breakfast she walked out the back door to find her granddad and brother working on the chicken coop.

"Well, Papa, look who finally got up?" Leroy said, laughing. "Gal, it sure is hot out—go fetch us a cold pail of water to drink,"

Paul said, pointing toward the pump near the big oak tree.

"Pump the water until it gets real cold, gal!" "Who made you boss, Leroy?" His sister asked.

"Hey, you two stop fussin'—it's too early to start all that craziness," Paul called out.

She just rolled her eyes at her brother and started pumping water into the pail, while they continued working on the coop. After delivering the water pail, she began handing Leroy nails. Before long, the noonday sun was beating down on them. Even after the cold water, they were still getting hot and hungry. Finally, taking a break, Paul started down the ladder, with Leroy following him. Leroy had taken just steps when he felt a tug on his pant leg—a nail had grabbed the cloth. He tried to bend over to release his pants from the nail, but as he shifted his weight on the ladder, the ladder started to sway, when Paul looked up as he felt the ladder giving way, it fell back with the two of them clinging for dear life as the ladder fell to the ground.

"Ouch! Help, Estella—come help us!" Her granddad shouted.

As she turned toward the coop, she was surprised to see her granddad lying on the ground with the ladder and her brother sprawled on top of him.

"Mama come help! Granddad and Leroy done fell off the ladder!"

She was able to lift the ladder off her brother, who started to get up slowly, but her granddad could not get up. She struggled to help him, yelling again, "Mama, come help!"

Julia came running from the house, still in her apron, as she had been preparing food for family to eat and take a break from their work in the hot sun. "What in the world done happened?" she asked.

As Julia ran to help, she could see Leroy trying to slowly stand up, but he cried out, "Ohhhhh Mama, help!" and fell back to the ground, grabbing his leg.

Paul thought he'd be able to help him, and reached up to grab Julia's hand, with his granddaughter on the other arm. At last Paul was standing, but poor Leroy was still on the ground, grabbing his leg and crying from the pain.

"How bad you hurt, boy?" His mother asked. "My leg, it's my leg!"

"Can you walk?"

"I don't know, Mama. It hurts bad, real bad!" "Here, boy, let me help you."

Leroy held out one hand to his sister and with the other hand reached out for his mother's shoulder. They both pulled hard and he was finally able to stand, but only on one leg. Hanging on to his sister and mother for support, he hopped on one leg back toward the house. Julia looked back to Paul following them, but he was still bent over with his hand on his back, showing a lot of pain in his face.

"You okay, Paul," she asked. "I reckon so."

Reaching the house, Paul and Leroy were able to make it over to the old worn-out sofa, near the front door. Julia reached over to pull her son's pant leg up. "You got a cut on your leg, boy, and it's bleeding a bit. It startin' to swell some, too. I think you need not to walk on that leg for a while."

"Mama, what we going to do for Papa's back?" "Why you asking her, gal? It's my back!"

Julia just smiled and decided to let them both rest and have Estella see about her granddad. She needed to check on the pies in the oven. They must be ready—with all the excitement, she nearly forgot about them.

"I'll see about them, Mama."

"Let me know if you need any help."

Julia walked back to the kitchen, checking on her pies; she noticed a wagon through the kitchen window coming down the road. She yelled into the front room, "It's that boy, Estella!"

Now that her brother and granddad were resting on the couch, she was free to run to the front door, opening it to see Zac climbing down from his wagon.

"How you doin', Estella?"

"Not so good; Papa and my brother done fell down off the ladder, buildin' on that old chicken coop. Leroy got a bad leg and Papa hurt his back. Come on in. Mama is fixin' dinner. I hope you can stay a while."

Zac followed her back into the house, seeing Julia inside and the two injured souls on the couch, he lowered his voice, almost whispering. "Hi Ms. Reynolds, sorry to hear about the accident."

"Yes, I think they will be fine. We goin' to let them rest. I'm fixin' dinner—you need a plate?"

"Yes, ma'am; that would be right nice of you."

Estella and Julia set the table, while Zac settled in the old wooden rocking chair nestled away in the corner of the front room.

"You better not let Papa see you in his chair—he ain't goin to like it, Zac!"

"Estella, let that boy alone; that chair been settin' there all day, empty."

Giving them a big smile, Zac replied, "Your mama on my side."
"Ain't no sides, boy, but there is things to be done. How about you put some wood in the stove, befo' dat fire get too low to cook on?"

"Yes, ma'am."

Zac quickly added the wood to the stove, and took a seat at the table for dinner. As they ate, they talked about school, family, and working in the field. Suddenly from behind them, a familiar voice from the other side of the room asked, "What y'all doin'?"

"About time you woke up, Papa," Estella said.

Startled by his Grandfather's voice, Leroy jumped to his feet, for- getting about his injured leg. "Owwww-ohhhh noooo! Ouch!"

"You better get off that leg, son! You ain't goin to be walkin' on it no time soon," Paul told him.

Leroy stumbled back onto the couch, holding his leg and wincing with pain.

"Y'all got dinner done yet," asked Paul.

"We ate a long time ago, Papa. Y'all been asleep fo' about three hours."

"Why you didn't call us, gal?"

"You needed to get some rest. I ain't babyin' y'all; I just want y'all to get better," Estella replied.

Leroy once again stood up—only this time, just on one leg. He hopped over to the table, followed by Paul, who was still bothered by the pain in his back.

Moving slowly toward the table, he asked, "Is that leg of yours still swollen, boy?"

Leroy pulled at his pant leg, and looked down. "A lot more, Papa!" In fact, it was so swollen that the boy could hardly pull the material back down over the swollen leg.

"Don't look like we are in shape to finish that there coop! Zac? How about you help us get it finished? Seein' how me and Leroy will be gettin' around a little slow."

"Sorry, Mr. Reynolds; I got to go to the field, but I'm guessing I can help out later today."

"Good, Zac—that's kind of you," Julia told him.

"How about gettin' Estella back to school? I ain't in no shape to get up and down on that wagon to take her! Can Zac take her back for us, Papa?" Leroy asked.

"Well, Zac, what you think? Estella can't miss school and get behind in her lessons," Paul said.

"Yes, Mr. Reynolds, I can take her back to Greenwood on Sunday after church. Okay?"

"That will be just fine! Thank you!"

"Well I best be goin'—before it gets too late. Thanks for the meal, Ms. Julia."

"I'll walk you out to the wagon, Zac." Estella added. "What time you get out of church, Estella?"

"Sometime we gets out round three o'clock, if the Reverend Lockwood don't give one of his long sermons. But if he gives one of his long sermons, it could be four or five o'clock fo' we gets out."
"Well then, I will come by the church about three o'clock and set in the back. Watch for me, so we can leave when I get up and walk out. Okay?"

"I don't know if the reverend or Papa will like me walking out of the service."

"Well then, tell your granddad what time I will be comin' to pick you up—that way he won't get mad when you walks out."

"That's a good idea," she told him, as he bent over and gave her a little kiss on the cheek. He quickly climbed onto the wagon. Estella watched him ride down the dusty road, until he disappeared into dusk's darkness.

The next day, after a long day in the field and hot sun, Zac returned to help Estella and her granddad with the chicken coop. Once again they worked until near sunset.

"Well folks, I best be gettin' down the road fo it gets too dark—ain't much light left now." Zac waved back to Estella. "I'll be back Saturday afternoon to help finish the coop."

Walking over to shake Zac's hand, Paul said, "I sho thank you, Zac, for all the help—my back is still givin' me some trouble."

"I'm happy to help y'all."

As Zac walked over to his wagon, Estella stopped him to plant a quick little kiss on his cheek. She felt very strange kissing a boy in front of her granddad. But, to her surprise, her granddad added, "Gal, that boy is pretty nice, and he sho helped me a lot with this coop. I know you kind of sweet on him."

Estella just smiled at her granddad, thinking only about Saturday afternoon when she would see Zac again. Saturday afternoon came before Estella knew it. Zac showed up just like he said. Estella waved as Zac walked over to help them finally finish the chicken coop.

"Glad to see you again, Zac," Paul said.

"Yes, I'm glad to see you too!" Estella chimed in with a big smile. They continued to talk and work in the hot sun, determined to finish the coop before noon. At last, Paul stepped away to look at the finished coop. Leroy sat on a nearby tree stump, telling the workers how sorry he was that he couldn't help, but his leg was still healing. Zac and Paul gathered the leftover materials. Zac said, "I'm not gonna be able to take Estella to Greenwood on Sunday. I have some things to do for my daddy on Sunday, but I can take her this afternoon."

"I'll check with her mama to see if that's okay," Paul told him, as they walked back to the small gray shack.

Julia was washing clothes in a big number ten washtub, under the big oak tree near the back of the house. Looking up from the washboard, Julia asked, "Y'all got that coop done yet?"

"We sho do, Julia! I think that chicken coop gonna be around longer than us," Paul said.

Just then Leroy came out the back door. "We sho put that wood from that old house that fell down to good use. We goin' to use the rest of that wood to put up an outhouse when my leg gets better."

Estella blurted out, "Mama, Zac ain't gonna be able to take me to Greenwood tomorrow, like he told you. But he is goin' to Greenwood this afternoon can he take me with him. Will that be all right with you?"

"What time you goin' to Greenwood, boy?"

"Well, ma'am, I have to go home and I can be back here about four o'clock to get Estella."

"I reckon it will be all right. Are you goin' to eat at your place, or come back here for dinner? If 'n you want me to fix you a plate, you can eat with us, fo' y'all go to Greenwood, just say so."

"Yes, ma'am; that would be mighty nice of you," Zac replied. Leroy just rolled his eyes at his mother, knowing that Zac coming for dinner meant no second helpings for him, like usual.

"I'll see y'all later." Zac replied, as he headed toward his wagon.

As the family returned to the house, they hoped it would not be too hot inside. Julia and Estella started dinner as Leroy and Paul swatted flies and mosquitoes, clearing the house of these pests; after a while, they found that killing bugs was only making them hot and sweaty.

"Girl, you better wash these greens, if you want to get dinner ready befo' that boy get back here Julia said."

"Mama," Leroy asked, "are you gonna bake an apple pie?"

But before Julia could answer, Estella yelled back, "He oughta make a pie if want one! It's too darn hot in dis house already!"

"Gal, ain't nobody talkin' to you!"

"Well, I am telling you it's too hot in here fo' pies!"

"Now you two stop fussin' and fightin'! Yes, son, I will make you a pie."

"You spoils him, Mama! He always get what he want!"

"There you go Estella, fussin' again! Hush, and fetch me some flour."

Before too long, dinner was ready, just in time—Estella could hear Zac's wagon outside; she ran outside to meet him. "I could smell your mama's apple pie befo' I got here," Zac explained.

They ate the food she had prepared; then Zac rose from the table, saying, "Now that was a good meal, Ms. Julia, but we better be gettin' down the road to Greenwood befo' it get too late."

"I guess you right, Zac. I hate to see Estella go back; but y'all best be on your way."

Estella went into her bedroom and picked up her books and clothes. They said their goodbyes and the family hugged. Paul handed her a box of food, saying, "Give this here food to the Jessup's, when you gets back to Greenwood."

Estella handed Zac her bags, books, and a basket of food her mother had prepared. Reaching down, Zac took her hand as she stepped up to take a seat next to him on the wagon. Turning back, as the wagon rolled down the dusty road to Greenwood, Estella waved and shouted, "'Bye, y'all!"

CHAPTER **14**

The Juke Joint

The heat of the day had passed and the afternoon air was a little cooler, as Zac guided the wagon down the road. Estella slid over on the wagon seat to be closer—her leg touching his.

"You like being close to me, gal?"

"I sho do!"

Zac smiled and wrapped his arm around her shoulder, pulling her even closer, as he guided the wagon with his other hand. The young girl looked up to see a very good-looking man. She could hear her heart beat a little faster—just like when she was in the picture show.

"Whooaaa!" Zac shouted, pulling back at the reins, bringing the wagon to a slow stop.

"Why we stopping here?"

Before she could say another word, he moved closer to her face and pressed his lips to hers. She felt his strong hand on the back of her head. He opened his mouth, pressing his tongue through her lips, until she opened her mouth. She had never felt this way, her heart beating like a drum, and her mind was spinning. She felt his hand on her back, finally releasing her from his strong arms. She was out of breath, from the long, deep kiss. Finally opening her eyes, he could see the pools of passion reflecting back at him.

"You sure got some good lips for kissin'," he whispered. But she could not muster a response. Zac just smiled and picked up the wag- on reins, slapping them on the backside of the mule, making the wagon jerk forward. A few miles down the road, Zac steered the wagon down a small side road.

"This ain't the way to Greenwood, Zac! Where you takin' me?"
"Now you just set there, and you goin' to find out soon enough."

She didn't know what to think, but she was worried about this side trip of Zac's. The road was very narrow, just wide enough for just one wagon at a time. Several times overhanging tree limbs would come close to hitting her as they traveled on. The sun was getting lower in the sky. She knew it would be dark soon, and she didn't know where he was taking her. Off in the distance she could hear what sounded like thunder, but there were no clouds in the sky. As their wagon continued down, the sound got louder.

"We been goin' down this here road a long time...Zac"

"We be gettin' there pretty soon, gal." Seeing some fear in her eyes, he tried to reassure her, "I think you gonna like it when we get there."

Her mind raced, where was "there," on this tiny road that she had never been down? And, it was getting darker and darker outside. The noise that once sounded like thunder was getting louder and louder.

"What is that noise, Zac?"

"You will see soon," Zac said, smiling at her.

Suddenly, she noticed a small lake to her left. The water was greenish-blue, and a light fog was rolling up from the surface into the late-afternoon air. Through the trees that surrounded the lake, she saw lights coming from what looked like an old rundown wood- en barn. Where and what was this place? At last, she could see where the sound was coming from. The noise was music—a band playing inside the barn.

"We is here!" Zac said, as he turned the wagon toward an open field filled with wagons and more people than Estella had seen since Easter Sunday at her church. Pulling back on the wagon reins, he found a spot to stop near the front of the barn. Estella had not in her life seen so many wagons of all sizes in one place, and off to one side of the open field were three automobiles.

She was so engaged in the sights and sounds that she didn't realize Zac had stepped down until she heard him say, "I think you goin' to like this here place," holding out his hand to help her down from the wagon. Estella took his hand, finding herself surrounded by dozens of people, smells, sounds, colors and movements that she had never seen before; all in one place. Inside the barn, the sound of the band was powerful. Through the open barn doors, she could see people dancing, both men and women dressed up like they were going to church.

They stood outside in a long line, where a big, heavyset man in gray overalls stood at the barn doors taking money from everyone that entered the barn.

"That will be twenty-five cents, boy," the big man told Zac, holding out his hand. Zac reached into his pocket and gave him a quarter. To the right of the entrance, Estella could see a man dressed in a white apron and chef's cap, standing over a big barrel of cooking meat of all kinds. There were chicken, ribs, pork chops, and sausage; and big pots of soup. Smoke filled the air around him. His white apron and chef's cap contrasted with his dark skin, the smoke making him appear to be in a gray fog.

"That sho do smell good, don't it, Estella?"

"Yes, but I hope all that smoke don't make him sick!" Zac just laughed. "I think he know what he's doin'."

As they walked into the barn, she noticed the barn had an upper loft, where people sat at tables, eating, drinking, and playing cards. There was a band playing under the big wooden planks of the barn loft; the rest of the barn's ground floor was filled with people dancing, moving up and down, back and forth, waving their arms, popping their fingers. Some women were swishing their skirts to the beat of the music.

"So, gal...how you like this place?"

"I like it ...but I ain't sure about the barn. Not so sure I should be here—we should be going back to Greenwood."

Zac didn't answer, but pointed to a man who wore a big derby hat and a nice black suit with a gold chain that hug across his vest, dripping across his middle, falling into his watch pocket. "This here is Big Ben, Estella—he owns this here place."

Estella looked at this big imposing man called Big Ben. She was afraid of him, but more surprised that a Negro man could own this place. Big Ben reached out toward Estella's hand, saying, "Who dis pretty young thing, boy?"

"This here is Estella, Ben."

"Well now, that sure be a pretty name to match a pretty gal!" Before Estella could pull back, Big Ben leaned forward, kissing the back of her nervous hand. "You a lucky young man, Zac, to have such a lovely girlfriend. It's been a week since I saw you last, boy."

"I wanted to come sooner, but I had to take care of some things at home," Zac replied.

"Well now, gal, I needs to speak with Zac a bit. I won't keep him too long, okay...pretty thing?"

Estella didn't get a chance to answer, before Zac turned to follow Big Ben around the back of the band stand. She took a few steps forward to keep her eyes on where the two men were going. Big Ben opened a small door to the left of the stage, as Zac and he entered. Luckily there was a small empty table with two chairs near that side of the bandstand, so she sat down. It was close to the band; the sound was overpowering, and the dancers seemed to be going faster and faster as the band played louder and louder.

Her mind started to roam; what could Zac be talking to Big Ben about? How did he know this big burly man, who owned this place? It was all so different from anything she had seen before. Just then Zac came out of the small room, with Big Ben behind him. Zac walked up to her table, holding out his hand. "Wanna dance?" Not waiting for her to reply, he took her by the hand and led her out to the dance floor among the crowd of people, doing dances she had never seen before.

"I don't know how to do these here dances!" She shouted to be heard over the loud music.

"Gal, just dance the way you know how. Ain't nobody payin' you no mind." She was very nervous, but decided to enjoy the music and being in Zac's arms. It seemed like only two minutes and suddenly the music stopped, causing people to slowly move toward the dozens of empty tables circling the dance floor.

As she and Zac walked back to their small table, she heard someone say, "Ladies and gentlemen...." It was Big Ben; he was standing on the stage in front of the band. "I have the honor of introducing someone you might know; the man from New Orleans, Mr. Louis Armstrong!"

The dance hall erupted into loud applause. The audience clapped for a long time; and when the applause stopped, a man carrying a bright shiny horn moved from behind the bandstand to the center of the stage.

"Thank you, ladies and gents! I'm happy to be here!"

Estella thought he was a little different-looking; he had big eyes, a broad smile, big lips, and a very raspy funny voice. He quickly started to blow his horn, and the place erupted again with loud applause; the crowd was calling out his name: "Louis, Louis!"

The sound of his horn filled the room; the band playing alongside him was the only other sound to be heard for some time. People were clapping, dancing, and having a good time. The music stopped; Louis dropped the horn from his mouth and started singing in a raspy, deep voice. The band played again, playing soft and low—as he sang, *All of me, take all of me.* His voice echoed throughout the barn. His next song, *"When You're Smiling,"* was Estella's favorite; she often heard her Grandfather singing and humming the song on their front porch.

Her thoughts of her Grandfather singing were interrupted by the applause of the crowd, as she saw Louis Armstrong bow to the crowd and walk off the stage. Big Ben returned to center stage, say- ing, "Well y'all that was the great Louis Armstrong! Ladies and gentlemen... the great Louis Armstrong!" The applause grew louder, and continued for several minutes.

At last Louis Armstrong reappeared from behind the stage. "Thank you, thank y'all for coming! It makes the trip from Chicago where I been playin' with the King Oliver Band worthwhile. I was on my way to New Orleans; but wanted to stop here to show my support for the owner of this place, Big Ben!"

Louis turned and put his arms around Big Ben, who was standing next to him; then he walked off the stage, hearing one last round of applause. Estella and Zac danced for a while after the performance. "Well, I sure am hungry, Estella, and thirsty—you want somethin' to eat?".

"I sho do—and that food sho smell good—-it's been cookin' for a while, makin' me hungry too!"

They walked over to the front of the barn where the man in the white apron and chef's cap stood surrounded by gray smoke. "What can I get for y'all?"

"Them ribs look good," Zac said, pointing to the meat on the pit. "How about you, gal?"

"I wants some chicken, please," Estella told the cook.

"Well, now, you got it!" He passed them each a plate piled high with ribs and chicken. "Here's some lemonade, too."

"Just give the bill to Big Ben," Zac told the cook, shocking Estella again. She really wanted to know what Zac knew or what he was doing, for Big Ben to be giving away free food. The cook gave Zac a small piece of paper to sign for their meal. After signing, Zac motioned Estella to follow him with her food. They soon stopped behind the barn. It was almost dark and the fireflies were flickering on and off near the edge of the lake. They found an old log near the water to sit on. Looking back, Estella could see the smoke from the pit and the mist from the lake forming together to make strangely shaped clouds that rose into the air.

The sound of the band playing in the background put magic in the air. But Estella's mind was still wondering about Zac and Big Ben. "How you know Mr. Big Ben, Zac?"

"I don't mean no harm, girl. But some things ain't good for you to know."

"It's okay if 'n you don't like me enough to tell me, Zac."

"It's not that I don't like you. It's just that it's for you own good that some things I don't tell you."

"Well, it gettin' mighty late—when are we going to start out for Greenwood?"

"In the mornin'."

"In the morning? I ain't going to stay here all night with you, Zac!"

"It's a little too late to be settin' out for Greenwood now," Zac laughed, looking in her eyes.

"But we ain't got nowhere to sleep!"

"Girl, don't worry about that. Big Ben got some rooms over yonder behind them trees," Zac said, pointing to a line of trees on the other side of the small lake. Estella could see a light coming through the trees. "We can stay in one of them cabins," he added.

"How you goin' to get a room, Zac?"

"I can tell Big Ben we need a room for the night. He owes me for some work I did for him."

"Zac, I don't know about staying with you in the same room."

Zac looked into her eyes once more, but this time he put his arms around her, holding her tight. She could feel the power in his strong arms.

"Gal, you ever been with a man before?" "What you mean, Zac?"

"I mean, have you ever slept with a man?" "No!" Estella blurted out.

"Well then, pretty girl, it's about time you do!" Zac pulled her closer and whispered in her ear.

Estella didn't know what to think or what to say next, and before she could say anything, Zac's lips were kissing her lips, making her heart beat faster. Her body was getting hot and sweaty, just like when Zac kissed her on the way to the show in Greenwood, and on the way here.

"I guess it will be okay," Estella whispered back, her words coming out in short, soft puffs. Zac stood up to give her his hand, so she could get to her feet.

"Come on then, gal—let's go back inside and I'll see if I can find Big Ben."

They walked back toward the barn. The music was still loud and the lights glowed through the old barn walls. Standing at the door, Estella was amazed by the dancers dressed in so many different colors—like a big moving flower, she thought.

She felt Zac pulling at her arm; turning toward him, she could see Big Ben walking from behind the bandstand. Zac motioned over to Big Ben.

"What you want with me boy?"

"I needs to talk to you alone in your office, Ben." "Sho nuf boy!"

"Okay, Estella, you wait here while I talks to Ben. I won't be long."

Estella sat down in the chair near the door to Ben's office, the same one she had sat in earlier. The door wasn't closed all the way. She couldn't see Zac, but Ben was facing the door, and she could hear both of them talking.

"Well, Zac, you got my goods?"

"I sho do, Ben—they in my wagon outside."

"Boy, you better not leave that moonshine out there too long—somebody could find it and walk away with all that there hooch and our money!"

106

THE ROAD FROM MONEY

"Ain't nobody goin to find it. It's under the seat, with lots of empty boxes in the front of it."

Now Estella knew how Zac and Big Ben knew each other. Ben was selling moonshine and Zac was bringing it to him. Selling moonshine could get them in lots of trouble if the Sheriff ever found out what they were doing, she thought. Just then the door opened, both men walked her way.

"Hey gal, you don't look like you havin' much fun sittin' there all alone!" Ben smiled down at her, holding out his hand. "How about a dance—if young Zac here don't mind?"

"It's okay by me," Zac replied.

Estella stood up, taking Ben's hand as they walked toward the dance floor. Zac watched the two of them for a moment, and then walked toward the barn entrance to his wagon to unload its cargo of moonshine. He quickly moved the empty boxes covering the two wooden boxes full of bottles, and walked toward the back of the barn, placing the boxes on the ground, as he quickly unlocked the shed door with a key Ben had given him in the office. Zac placed the boxes next to the other supplies in the shed. Locking the door behind him, he then re-entered the barn.

Estella walked over to him, saying, "That Big Ben is a very good dancer!" Zac took her hand, pulling her toward the dance floor again, only this time, he pulled her close to him. Estella's head resting on Zac's shoulder, they swayed to the soft music, along with the other dancers. Zac soon leaned down and whispered in her ear, "I got the key from Ben to one of his cabins." She just looked up into his eyes and smiled.

They danced for a short time before Zac asked if she was ready to go.

"I guess so," she replied.

The two of them walked off the dance floor and out the barn door into the clear night air, Zac taking the nervous young girl by the hand as they moved toward a row of small wooden cabins. Estella counted eight of them near the edge of the small lake, with fog rising off the lake as if it were a tub of hot water. The sound of frogs and crickets filled the air, with a light breeze carrying a slight smell of fish blowing across the lake.

Estella noticed each shack had a number painted on the door. Zac stepped up on the landing of No. 3, took a key from his pocket, and opened the door. The room was tiny, with only a bed and two chairs. Zac entered the room ahead of Estella. Walking over to the window, he glanced back at the very nervous young girl, saying, "I sure hope this window opens, 'cause it is hot in here. The breeze will help cool it down a bit."

Estella was not thinking about what Zac was saying. She could only think about being alone with him. Before she knew it, Zac was kissing and touching her body. Before the night was over, she would experience many feelings for the first time. She was afraid, but yet eager to feel what she overheard her mama and other women talk about—being with a man, becoming a woman.

The next morning Estella rolled over, opening her eyes, to hear Zac say, "Good morning, sleepy head."

"Good morning." She smiled back. "What we goin' to do now?" Reaching for his pants and shirt, Zac responded with a chuckle,

"Well, I reckon we walk back to the barn and get some breakfast!"

Estella grabbed her dress, as Zac walked over to a small tub in the corner of the room that had a black steel water pump over it. He pumped the long handle until the water was clear and rushing from the spout. They each formed a cup with their hands, catching some of the cold water, splashing it on their faces, sipping some of the water and spitting it out to help clean their mouths.

"This water sure do feel good!" Estella told Zac.

"It sho do—but I needs some breakfast. We best be gettin' down to the barn. That cook always got something on the stove."

"You come here a lot?"

"No, gal—not a lot, but sometimes."

Estella knew he wasn't telling the truth, because of what she had overheard outside of Big Ben's office. For the first time, she didn't know if she could trust Zac. Why did he say he didn't come here a lot, if he was running moonshine to Big Ben? As they walked back to the barn, she knew the questions would have to wait; she was hungry, and the smell of bacon cooking filled the air as they got closer to the barn. Zac opened the door for her to enter. It was much different from the night before. She saw only a few people at the tables eating and talking.

Big Ben sat at one of the tables with two women, who were dressed as if they were still on the dance floor or ready for church. She also noticed that he was smiling and having a good time, laughing loudly and waving his hands in the air. One of the women stood up and placed her hands on her hips, shaking her head from side to side, laughing.

"Looks like Big Ben havin' a good time with those gals!" "It sho do," Estella agreed.

Ben looked up and motioned for them to come over to his table. "Hey you two, I want you to meet Joy and Mary; they good friends of mine!" Ben stood up, giving Estella a big hug, and the two women gave Zac a hug.

"I bet y'all hungry!" Ben said, winking at Zac.

"We sho is!" Zac said, rubbing his stomach. "I think I could eat a whole pig by myself!"

"Y'all pull up a chair and have a seat. I'll tell Bob to fix y'all something to eat. You ain't had no cookin' 'til you eat Bob's cookin', gal," Ben said.

The man Estella had seen cooking outside the barn the night before entered from a side door behind them. Ben motioned for him to come over. "You need something, boss?" Bob asked.

"I needs you to rustle up a big breakfast for these two young folks," Ben told him.

"Yes, boss!" Bob replied, as he disappeared into the kitchen, re- turning later with a tray full of bacon, eggs, pancakes, fruit, and some homemade jelly.

"This sho do look good, Mr. Bob," Estella said, looking up at him.

"Thank you, ma'am. You wants anything else, boss," Bob asked Ben.

"No Bob, you done just fine, like you always do," Ben replied. "No problem, boss. Y'all young folks enjoy your breakfast." Bob winked at Estella, and walked back toward the side door.

"Y'all enjoy this here food—I needs to go plan tonight's show," Ben told them.

Zac and Estella sat for some time, eating and talking about their families, Estella's new school, and how badly Negroes got treated by white people. Most of all they wondered why their family and other Negroes in Money had to work so many hours in the field, live in such run-down shacks, and go to school that didn't have many books, and was a church on Sunday.

"One day, Zac, I'm gonna go North; 'cause'n it has got to be better than here," Estella said.

"Yes, Estella, I wants to go North too, but right now this is where I be."

"I know, Zac, but this ain't no place for nobody that wants good things like a pretty house, good schoolin', money in their pocket, and maybe one of them new automobiles—like we see sometimes on the road to Greenwood."

"Now gal, don't be silly! You know ain't no Negroes goin' to get no car here or up North. You know a car cost more than we ever goin' to be able to make!"

"That's why I be going to school in Greenwood," Estella said, laughing. "You wait and see—one day Negroes goin' to have as much as white folks."

Ben's familiar voice interrupted their conversation. "I gots a package for you, Zac." He handed Zac a big envelope. "I hope this be enough for your delivery, boy?"

Looking inside the envelope, Zac nodded. "This be just fine!"

"Well, then, when you coming back this way again, boy?"

"In about a week, Ben—that okay?"

"That sound just fine; y'all have a good ride home." Before he could say thank you, Ben had disappeared into his office, just behind the stage.

"Okay, Estella, we best be gettin' on the road again. We got a ways to go 'til Greenwood." Zac held out his hand to her, and soon the two of them were standing outside the barn, within just a few feet of their wagon. Estella saw Zac's mule eating oats and drinking water from buckets. Bending down, Zac picked up the two buckets and placed them next to a nearby tree.

"I think he's good and full now." Zac jumped up on the wagon seat, and held out his hand for Estella to pull her up next to him. It was almost noon; the sun was getting high in the sky. Estella took a big sun hat from under the wagon seat it was like the one she sometimes wore in the cotton fields to shade her face from the sun. Finally they were back on the road to Greenwood. It had been a night and day Estella would never forget.

CHAPTER **15**

The Storm

t had been nearly an hour since they left Big Ben's barn, when Zac pointed ahead, saying, "Looks like a storm cooking up yonder." Estella could see dark clouds off in the distance. "I hope it don't rain before we gets to Greenwood." They continued down the nar- row road, watching the clouds ahead turn from gray to black; the wind was blowing the trees harder and harder. Estella finally took her hat off and placed it under the seat before the wind sent it flying down the road behind them.

"Ain't goin to be long now fo' we gets to Greenwood gal." Zac slapped the reins harder, trying to make the mule go faster.

Estella noticed that the once-bright sky above them was starting to darken. Big black and gray clouds were above them and the air smelled like rain was on the way. Looking ahead, she could see a buckboard coming toward them. As it grew closer, they saw a well-dressed white man and woman. Their buckboard was pulled by two black horses that reminded her of pictures she had seen in books. And their buckboard had a roof that covered their heads. As it passed, she noticed the roof had little strings hanging all around the edge that swayed in the wind. She had seen strings like that on a fancy woman's dress in a catalog she saw at the Greenwood general store. Her mama had called it fringe. The woman waved at them as they passed. The man holding the reins just stared straight ahead, as if he didn't see them or their wagon.

"Now that there is some kind of wagon! I thinks that wagon almost good-lookin' as one of them automobiles, and almost as fast!"

"It throws up too much dust," Estella said.

As they continued on, the sound of distant thunder made Zac stop talking about the buckboard. He knew he had to get their mule moving faster, and they had to find someplace to get out of the on- coming storm. Just then, a flash of lightening lit up the sky. It was still some distance from them, but getting closer. Zac slapped the reins on the backside of the mule, as he struggled to keep ahead of the coming storm.

"I don't like being out in the open, when it lightning and thunder." Estella told him.

"We ain't goin' to make it to Greenwood; this here storm is com- ing too fast! We need to find a dry place and let it pass us. I knows where there is an old house where nobody lives, up the road a bit." Before she could reply, she felt raindrops on her arms, and knew he was right.

Zac quickly turned their wagon onto a narrow road. Estella thought it looked much like the road they had taken to Big Ben's place. She didn't know what to think, but she was nervous. The rain was coming down good now; she didn't know how he could see. The thunder and lightning were getting closer and closer, when she no- ticed an old rundown house just a few feet away. Even through the storm, she could see that bricks from the house were lying all around the yard, and most of the windows were broken or missing. At least the roof looked all right for now, she thought.

"Let's get inside," Zac called out, jumping down from the wagon, and reaching out to Estella. He practically lifted her from the wagon seat. Grabbing her hand, he pulled her toward the porch of the house, and through the wooden door that had fallen off its hinges onto the porch.

"We got here just in time—Zac." Looking up she could see that there must have been a fire in the old house; most of the inside walls were charred and black.

Zac looked around trying to find a safe place for them to take shelter, still holding on to Estella's hand. He noticed a corner of the house, next to a big beam that seemed to be sturdy enough for them to hold on to. He pulled Estella into the corner and held her close. He thought how pretty she was, just as a bright flash lit up her pretty face. The storm was right above them now. Loud claps of thunder seemed to explode one on top of another.

Suddenly, it sounded like small rocks were being thrown at the house. Zac knew it was hail, but was more concerned about the wind; it was starting to sound like a train coming down the track toward them. Zac looked out the window on the other side of the room, seeing boards, bricks, and trees blowing past them. Estella shook with fear in his strong arms, as the storm raged all around them.

"Don't let go of me, Zac!" She shouted. Zac held her tight as the world around them seemed to be coming apart. It seemed like a long time, but just as suddenly as the storm had started, the wind was dying down and the rain had nearly stopped. Once again he looked over at the window and was surprised to see the sun coming out from behind a big white cloud, as the storm continued on to the North.

"Look, Zac—it's the sun!"

"Yes, I see it...time we get out of here!"

They walked out the front door onto what was left of the porch to see what the storm had done. They saw trees lying in the front yard everywhere, and the house had lost most of its roof, another wall, and the chimney that had been standing when they arrived.

"Where's the mule and our wagon go?"

Estella had been so frightened that she had forgotten about the wagon and the mule. She thought Zac had tied them up to a tree near the house. But there were no trees standing now, and she wondered if the mule would even be alive after that awful storm.

"Look—there's the mule—and the wagon too—over yonder in that there field." Zac pointed toward the field across from the old house. They both ran across the small yard, into the field about fifty feet away.

"I hope the wagon and mule be all right! That was one bad storm!"

"I think that there storm was a tornado, gal!"

As they reached the wagon, Zac walked slowly up to the mule, not wanting to scare him more than he was already. Reaching down, he pulled the mule's reins from the mud. The field was muddy in spots, and had standing water in other places. He jumped up on the wagon seat, and pulled Estella up next to him. Slapping the mule with the reins, he was ready to finally finish their trip to Greenwood. But no matter how hard he slapped the reins on the mule's behind, the wagon didn't move. He jumped down from the wagon, to find that all four wagon wheels were covered deep with mud.

"Get down, gal—we ain't goin nowhere right now; we got to make this here wagon lighter so the mule can pull it."

As Estella stepped down, being careful not to fall in the mud, Zac gave her the reins to hold.

"Now, when I push on the back of the wagon, you pull them reins hard as you can." Finally, after about an hour of pushing and

116

pulling, slipping and sliding, at last the wheels were on dryer ground. Estella was glad to see the wagon free and jumped up on the wagon seat, eager to be back on the road to Greenwood. "Hey gal, don't get back on the wagon yet. We got to walk the mule and wagon back to the road. There is too much mud; we could get stuck again."

Walking slowly, they were able to steer the wagon and mule back to the road, and out of the wet, muddy field. At last, they were able to climb aboard and head to Greenwood.

The sun was shining bright and hot; as they continued on down the road they saw big trees up- rooted, fallen tree limbs, and boards lying everywhere that had been tossed around like feathers.

"We sho lucky that storm didn't kill us, Zac!"

He didn't answer her right then; he was more concerned about the tree lying across the road ahead of them.

Estella saw the tree across the road too. "Now what we gonna do?"

Zac looked around to see if he could go around the tree, but there was a small creek full of water from the storm on one side, and on the other, a field full of mud.

"I got an axe that I keeps in the back of the wagon; if I can cut off some of them limbs, maybe we can push the tree off the road."

Zac jumped down and pulled the axe from the wagon, and began chopping limbs from the tree. Estella helped by pulling the braches to the edge of the muddy field. For the next hour, the two worked together to finally clear enough of the branches from the fallen tree, to allow the wagon to pass.

"Good thing the bottom of the tree didn't fall this way, or I would still be chopping," Zac said.

"I hope there ain't no more trees across the road ahead," she replied.

117

CHAPTER 16

The Wagon Wheel

As Estella and Zac traveled down the road, they saw a lot of damage from the storm—houses without roofs, walls missing, and trees lying across houses, porches, and barns. Every so often they would see a cow, a horse, and a few chickens roaming around free. Estella started to think about the Jessups, and what the storm might have done to their house.

Looking up the road Zac saw a man standing in the road, waving his arms above his head, walking toward them.

"Help! Help! My wife got hit by a tree limb, and she's bleeding bad! She's got to get to the hospital in Greenwood; please!" The man shouted.

Zac jumped from the wagon, following the man—finding a woman lying in the back yard, blood coming from her head. She was moving her arms up to her face, trying to wipe the blood away from her eyes.

"Can she walk?" Zac asked.

"Dear, can you get on your feet and walk," he asked his wife. "I think so," she answered.

The man grabbed one arm and motioned for Zac to help with the other, pulling the woman to her feet, only to almost fall back to the ground. Zac was the stronger of the two, and was able to catch her as she started to fall. Estella looked on as they lifted the injured woman into the old wagon. Taking a clean handkerchief from her purse, Estella folded the small cloth and handed it to the stranger. "This might help," she added. The man was very surprised at the gesture, and handed the handkerchief to his wife.

"Thank you," the woman moaned to Estella, as she placed the cloth to her wound.

"Yes, ma'am," Estella answered.

"I know this wagon ain't goin nowhere, if 'n we all get on. One mule can't pull all four of us and the wagon too," Zac told them.

"What we gonna do?"

"The man said he would walk behind the wagon." "I can walk too, Zac," Estella added.

As the wagon with Zac and the women started down the narrow road, it started moving much faster than Estella and the man could walk. "The wagon is too far ahead of y'all!" Zac called back. "I don't want to get too far ahead! What if someone come down this road, and see me with a white woman bleeding in the back?"

"Boy, don't you worry 'bout that—just get my wife to the hospital in Greenwood!"

Zac and the injured woman pulled slowly away from Estella and the stranger; in minutes, they could barely see the wagon.

"I hope your wife is all right," Estella told the man as they walked down the road.

"God, I hope so too, gal!"

Just then the man noticed the wagon had stopped about 100 feet ahead of them. "Now what, boy?" he shouted, as he ran ahead to see why they had stopped. Estella followed him as best she could, hear- ing the man say, "Oh no!"

Looking up, Estella saw that the wagon was in the middle of the road, leaning to the right, with one wheel on the ground. Zac was standing with his hands on his hips, just looking at the broken wheel.

"We gots to get my wife some help!"

"Look!" Estella shouted, pointing toward a carriage coming up the road. It was the same wagon they had seen earlier before the storm.

"My God!" the man added, as the big carriage, being pulled by two black horses, grew closer. Finally, it came to a full stop behind the broken wagon.

"Whoa, whoa! What's going on here?" the carriage driver asked, seeing the broken wheel and the woman in the back, bleeding.

Rushing over to the carriage, the man told the carriage driver that his wife had been hit by a tree limb during the storm. "I need to get my wife some help; can you help me get her to Greenwood?"

"Yes, y'all need to get her in here fast!"

Zac helped the man lift his wife from their broken-down wagon and onto the seat behind the driver. Zac and Estella watched as the carriage started to pull away, and then stopped suddenly. The driver's wife called back to them, "Don't y'all just stand there—jump in. There's enough room for everyone."

They were both surprised and glad to hear the woman's offer for a ride to town. Zac knew he needed more than Estella's help to fix a broken wagon wheel; he quickly grabbed a bag from under the wagon seat, and helped Estella up into the carriage.

The carriage driver called out, "Getty up, getty up!" Shaking the reins, the carriage jumped forward as the two big horses galloped toward town.

Estella had never felt anything move so fast. The driver shook the reins again, and the carriage moved even faster. The injured woman sat up, holding her head. "Where am I," she asked.

"You just lay back down," her husband said, trying to comfort her. Estella noticed the woman's head wound had almost stopped bleeding. Looking outside the carriage, she recognized some of the houses and buildings along the road. She was sure they must be close to Greenwood, but didn't see much damage from the storm—only a few trees blown over, or branches down. It was nothing like the damage out in the countryside, just a few miles outside of town.

"You two jump off, we in Greenwood," the driver's wife called back to Zac and Estella. The carriage slowed down, but didn't stop completely. Zac jumped down first and was careful to make sure Estella didn't fall. In just seconds, the carriage pulled away.

"I hope that white woman be okay, Zac."

"Yes, me too—but we need to get to the Jessup house before dark."

"I'm glad that storm didn't hit Greenwood, like it did back yonder!"

It took nearly a half-hour for them to finally see Carl and Ann Jessup in the front yard looking at their house, examining the damage from the storm. As they entered the small yard, stepping over branches, Estella yelled out, "Hi y'all!"

Carl and Ann looked very surprised to see the two familiar faces coming toward them. Ann grabbed Estella, hugging her hard, looking behind her, but not seeing Zac's old wooden wagon. "What happened? Where is your wagon, Zac?" Ann asked.

"The wheel done come off that old wagon about two miles south of town."

"Well, then, come on in the house. I am just happy to see y'all! That was a bad storm that come through! But how did y'all get away from that storm, being out on the road and all? We were lookin' for y'all a little later."

"We left early from Money, when the storm started. We stood inside an old rundown farm house, where nobody lives!"

"Where that wagon be of yours, boy? Is it on the road between here and Money?" Carl asked.

"Yes, sir; about two miles south of town."

"Well, if we leave now, I can pick up Ruth and see 'bout fixin' that wagon of yours. I know you just got here but I want to see if I can fix that wagon wheel."

"Thanks, Carl; maybe the two of us can get it done."

The two men loaded the Jessup wagon with wood blocks and a few tools, and started back toward Greenwood to fix the wagon. Ann and Estella sat on the front porch, talking about the storm, and how Estella was doing in school. As the afternoon turned into dusk, they went into the house to prepare the dinner, thinking the men would return soon.

"It's been some time since them men left. I sho hope they be all right, Estella."

Not wanting to seem worried, Ann asked Estella to slice some bread for the table and fetch fresh water from their well outside. Another hour passed, and dusk was turning to darkness.

"I don't know what's taking them so long," Ann said.

"They be all right—they got to stop to fetch Ruth and then fix Zac's wagon," Estella replied.

As they continued to cook dinner, Ann stood at the kitchen sink, facing a window that looked down the road to Greenwood. Finally, a few minutes later, she saw not one but two familiar wagons coming up the road to their house. She turned and smiled at Estella, saying, "I told you not to worry, gal. I can see them coming now."

Ann and Estella walked outside to see Carl and Zac steering both wagons up to the Jessup house. Ruth was riding next to Carl.

"Sorry we took so long!" Carl said, jumping down from the wagon, with Ruth stepping down next to him; giving Ann a big hug. "We had a time with that wheel, and that mule of mine ain't feelin' so good; he be too old to be pullin' that wagon in this here heat. I hope we can get another mule before he go down."

"Y'all can wash up, while Estella and I set the table. I know y'all must be hungry."

"Tired and hungry," Zac replied.

"Well then, let's eat. You know the girls need to get to bed; they got school tomorrow."

Estella and Ruth wanted to talk more about the storm, but it had been a long day and afternoon for everyone.

CHAPTER 17

The Test

The next day for Estella and Ruth started early. When they heard the front door of the house close loudly as Carl left for work, they knew it was time to get ready for school. As they dressed, the smell of ham and eggs filled the air. They quickly ate their breakfast, grabbed the lunch bags Ruth had prepared, and ran out the door to walk just over a mile to school. Just a few minutes away from the Jessup house, Estella noticed a gray-haired white woman sitting on the front porch of a large white house. The yard was lined with trees on each side and baskets of flowers hung from the porch columns.

Estella saw the woman wave at them—it was odd, she thought, for a white person to live so near the Negro part of town. Most white people lived on the other side of the train tracks, where Negroes worked as servants, but didn't live in Greenwood.

"You know that woman," Estella asked.

"No, but she always waves when I go by; she ain't like most white folk."

The girls continued walking until they could hear their noisy classmates in the play yard. As they entered the school's door, they saw Mrs. Williams coming down the hall. Ruth's classroom was just a few feet away. Reaching the door, she opened the classroom door to enter the room.

Estella looked up to see Mrs. Williams again, who said, "I need to talk to you, young lady; not now, but after school."

"Yes, Mrs. Williams." *She wondered—had she done something wrong?* Not knowing what else to say, she continued on to her classroom at the end of the hallway. It was the first day of school after summer break. She was excited to see her friends and teachers, but in the back of her mind, she also wondered why Mrs. Williams wanted to see her after school. When the school bell rang at the end of the day, Estella headed to Mrs. Williams' office, stopping to knock at her door.

"Come in," she heard Mrs. Williams say. As she opened the of- fice door, she saw Mrs. Williams looking at her over her glasses. "Have a seat," she told Estella.

"Yes, ma'am."

"How was your time away from school?"

"I had a good time, being with my family and friends in Money."

"That's good. The reason I called you to my office is that I no- ticed at your age, you should be out of sixth grade. I have good news for you—if you can pass a test, I am going to let you graduate with

the eighth grade class, at the end of this school year."

She could not believe what Mrs. Williams was telling her. She was going to be able to graduate the eighth grade with the next class, if she could pass a test!

"You may want me to help you study after school, so you can pass the test."

Estella smiled, wanting to run up and hug Mrs. Williams. "That's all. You can go now, Estella."

"Yes, ma'am," she mumbled, still sitting in the office chair across from her school's headmistress.

"You can go now, young lady," Mrs. Williams repeated.

Estella stood up with tears in her eyes, walked behind the large wooden desk, bent over, and gave the surprised woman a big hug around the neck. "Thank you! Thank you! Mrs. Williams!" She quickly stepped away; hearing Mrs. Williams chuckle as she walked out the office into the hallway, taking a handkerchief from her pocket to wipe away her tears of joy.

Estella looked up the hallway to see Ruth coming toward her. "Guess what, Ruth? I am going to graduate with you this year!"

"How you going to do that? Why you crying, Estella?" "Mrs. Williams going to move me up, if I can pass a test!" "That's great!" Ruth said, giving her a big hug.

"I can't wait to tell my mama and Grandfather...everyone in Money gonna be surprised!"

The girls ran out the school door, arm in arm, laughing and talk- ing about how they would study hard together to help Estella pass the test, and how happy she would be to move up two grades to graduate with Ruth.

Over the next few months, Estella studied each Monday after school with Mrs. Williams and each night with Ruth. Sometimes the lessons and books she read were hard for her to understand. With the help of Mrs. Williams and Ruth, she was doing better and better as the weeks and months ran by. As fall turned into winter and finally spring, she was feeling more and more confident that she could pass the test. School was ending and graduation was just two weeks away, and at last, the day of Mrs. Williams' test was here.

Entering the school, Estella saw Mrs. Williams in the hall, she asked, "What time do you want me to come to your office to take the test?"

"Do you think you are ready for the test, Estella?" "I think I is, Mrs. Williams."

"It is not 'I think I is,' Estella," she told the girl. "You should say, 'I think I am.'"

"Yes, ma'am," Estella replied, lowering her head slightly. Walking over to Estella, the woman reached out to gently lift the girl's head up, and added with a big smile, "I think you will do just fine. Come back to my office after your last class."

As instructed, Estella walked into Mrs. Williams' office after her last class. As usual, Mrs. Williams was sitting behind her desk. She looked up as Estella entered the room.

"Estella, I've been waiting for you. We need to get this test out of the way." Reaching down, Mrs. Williams opened her desk drawer and took out what seemed to be about six or seven sheets of paper. Placing them on the small table across from her desk and motioning to Estella, she said, "Please have a seat."

"Yes, ma'am."

Mrs. Williams handed her the papers. Estella was so excited; her head was spinning. She knew if she didn't pass the test, she could not graduate at the end of the year. She could not let that happen. She must pass this test. Mrs. Williams could see how nervous the girl was. She could see sweat on her brow.

"You'll do just fine, Estella. Please begin."

Estella didn't say a word. She reached for her pencil and stared at the first page. She read the first question, and to her surprise, she knew the answer. Letting out a deep breath, she now had the feeling that she was going to pass the test after all. Over the next forty-five minutes she tackled each page and each question, thinking long and hard on the answers.

"Time is up," Mrs. Williams said, breaking the silence. Estella had only one more question to answer, when Mrs. Williams told her the test was over. She handed her the test that she had worked so hard to complete, to finally graduate. Mrs. Williams smiled at her as she took the test papers from her hand, and Estella remained seated at the small desk in the corner.

"I hope I did good on this here test."

"We don't say 'this here test,' Estella. We say 'this test.'" "Yes, ma'am."

Mrs. Williams took the test back to her desk, to review the answers. As she watched her review the pages, she was very nervous, wondering if she was going to get enough of the answers correct. Finally Mrs. Williams looked up over her glasses, something she did often, saying, "Estella, I have good news for you. Your grade is ninety percent; you missed only four questions. I knew you could do it!"

Estella was overjoyed; this was the best thing that had ever happpened to her. She couldn't wait to tell Ruth that she passed the test. "Thank you, Mrs. Williams! Thank you! Thank you!"

"No need to thank me—you did it," Mrs. Williams said. "But I couldn't have done it without you...Mrs. Williams!"

"Well, thank you, Estella. I think you have a graduation to prepare for, and you should share this good news with your family too."

"Oh yes, ma'am! I will tell everyone!"

Mrs. Williams laughed and walked up to Estella to give her a hug. The girl was surprised and nearly in tears. She didn't want Mrs. Williams to see her so emotional, and turned to open the door. "I'll see you at the graduation; you and your family, I imagine."

"Yes, thank you again." Estella bolted out the door to find Ruth, who had been waiting for her to take the test. She was outside Mrs. Williams' office when Estella walked out into the hall.

Ruth ran toward her, saying, "How did it go?" "I passed! I passed the test!"

Ruth hugged her tight, saying, "We must tell the family!" "I can't wait to tell everyone!" Estella shouted.

CHAPTER 18

Miss Bertha's Story

Arm in arm, the two girls ran out the schoolhouse door and down the road to the Jessup house. Along the way, they passed the big white house; like most days, the woman was sitting on a white wicker rocking chair. As they got closer, the woman walked to the fence and shouted out, "How y'all doin'? Every day I see you girls going to school. I hope you can stop and talk one day; we can have something cold to drink."

The girls always thought it was a little strange for this woman to be on the porch almost every day as they passed on their way to school. She always waved, but this was the first time she had spoken to them. "Maybe you can visit another time, after you ask your folks. What are your names?"

"I'm Estella, and this here is…I mean, this is Ruth."

"It's nice to finally meet you both. My name is Bertha Johnson, but they call me Miss Bertha."

"Well, Miss Bertha, we better be gettin' on home," Estella said, as she pulled on Ruth's arm. "Let's go, Ruth," she whispered to

Ruth. "'Bye, Miss Bertha," the two girls said in unison, as they ran off toward home.

"What you think about Miss Bertha, Estella?"

"I don't know; I think she always watching us, and that makes me feel funny."

"Why you think she wants to talk to us again?" "Don't know, but maybe we gonna find out."

The rest of the way home, they talked about Miss Bertha. Before they knew it, they could see the Jessup house, with Ruth in the front yard, watering the flowers. "Hello Auntie," Ruth said.

"I was getting worried about y'all," her Aunt replied.

"We stopped to talk to the old gray-haired white woman that live in the big house by the train track."

Her Aunt scowled, saying, "Why y'all talkin' to that woman?" "She stopped us on the way from school and wanted us to come back to visit. Can we go?"

"What that woman want to talk to you about?" "We don't know," Estella told her.

"She look nice enough, Auntie."

"I wonder why she live on this side of the train tracks, where us Negroes live? Most white folk don't wanna be around us. But if you gals want to go see that old woman, you need to go now. Just be back here before dinnertime."

"Yes, Ma'am." Ruth replied.

Estella and Ruth ran quickly into the small house, placing their books on the table near the front door. As the girls walked into the front yard, Ruth looked up from pulling weeds from the flower bed. "Y'all get back here in time for dinner, now. And mind you don't let your supper get cold."

"Yes, Ma'am."

The girls continued on down the road, talking about the old white woman they would see. "Ruth, you think that old lady got lots of money?"

"I don't know. That house she lives in is so big, and she's the only one I see living in there."

As they reached the house, they didn't see the woman sitting on the porch in her white wicker rocking chair. Opening the front gate, they moved toward the house down a flower-lined path. The closer they got to the blue front door of the house, the more Estella started to think that this might not be such a good idea.

"You think we ought to turn around and go home?"

"Well, you wanted to come here as much as I did, Estella." The girls continued on, climbing up the porch stairs. The rocking chair where Miss Bertha usually sat seemed to be moving by itself; actually it was being pushed by the wind.

"This here house is kind of spooky," Estella said, after seeing the chair move.

"This house ain't spooky—it's just big and pretty," Ruth replied, as she knocked on the front door. They were both shocked to see a gray-haired Negro man open the door.

"What can I do for you," he asked.

"We're here to see...." Before Ruth could finish, the man interrupted her.

"Please come in," he told them, stepping aside, motioning them to enter. He closed the door behind them and added I think, "Miss Bertha is expecting you gals. She will be down soon. Please have a seat in the parlor."

The girls walked into the parlor. Ruth sat in one of two beautiful red velvet chairs near a large window; Estella sat across from her in a small tufted gold sofa. Touching the fabric, Estella knew the woman had to be rich; she had never seen or felt such soft fabric be- fore. There were little golden threads stitched around the sofa cushions, causing them to almost sparkle from the afternoon sun coming through the window.

"This here is the biggest house I've ever been in," Estella said, looking around the room at all the elegant furniture and the vase on the table in front of her. Just then, Miss Bertha entered the room, taking a seat in other red velvet chair next to Ruth.

"I was hoping you gals would come back to visit for a while. I'll have James bring us some lemonade." She called out and moments later James entered the room standing straight and tall; dressed in black pants, white shirt, with a black bow tie and white gloves. They hadn't noticed until now that he was Ms. Bertha's butler.

"Yes, Miss Bertha."

"James, would you get us some lemonade right away?"

"Yes ma'am, right away." James turned and walked away quickly. "Now, how you gals doin' in school?"

"We're doin' good," they answered, together. "That's good I like to see our folks do good."

The two girls looked at each other, both thinking that this old lady was crazy and maybe they should get out of this place. Seeing how puzzled the girls looked, her face lit up with a big smile. "I am Negro, just like you gals."

Estella looked at Ruth, not knowing what to say or think. *How is this here white woman goin' be a Negro?* Estella wondered. This was the funniest thing they had ever heard.

"Before you girls think I've lost my mind, let me tell you a story," Bertha added.

Just then James returned with a pitcher of lemonade on a serving tray with three glasses, placing it on the small table between the sofa and two chairs. "Thank you, James; that will be all." With that, James turned and left the room. Estella was thinking maybe she shouldn't drink the lemonade; this Bertha woman might have put something in it.

"Before we enjoy a cool drink, let me show you girls the rest of the house."

Bertha rose to her feet and pointed to the door, motioning for them to follow her into the next room. They were amazed at how large this house was; they walked through room after room, and none of them were small. Each room was a different color and the furniture was the best they had ever seen, not like the homemade furniture she had seen in Money, or even in Greenwood. Negroes she knew never had such beautiful things, she thought. Bertha opened the door to a room that had been locked, but all the other rooms were open. Once the door opened, they saw pictures of people hanging on a wall in front of them. Looking at the pictures, Estella noticed that some of the people in the pictures were Negroes, and others were white.

"This is my family; all the people you see in these pictures are related to me." The girls could not believe their eyes and were shocked and surprised at what Miss Bertha was telling them. She pointed to a picture of a Negro woman, saying, "This woman is my grandmother. And the man in this picture here is my daddy, and the woman next to him is my mother."

They had not seen or heard anything like this before—a white woman with a Negro grandmother, a white papa, and a Negro mother. How could this be? They wondered.

134

"Well, what do you think about these pictures and the people in the pictures?"

"You got a nice family," Ruth mumbled.

"Lord have mercy; now I done see everything. A white woman who got a Negro grandmother that says she's Negro!" Estella blurted out, in a loud voice.

Miss Bertha just laughed, saying, "Let's go back to the parlor and I'll tell you something about me and my family. Once in the parlor Miss Bertha said have a seat, and help yourselves while we talk. I know you're wondering how I look so white, when my grandmother is Negro. Well, back in slavery time my grandmother's master had his way with her and my mother was born. When my mother was a young woman, she worked as a maid in a big house owned by a wealthy family. When his wife died the white man, who was the owner of the house, took my mother as his lover. And two years later

I was born and the wealthy white man was my father. My mother was very light-skin, and since my father was white, I look almost white. Only my nose and lips I got from my grandmother. I am a Negro, just like you two."

Estella and Ruth looked at Miss Bertha and wondered why she was telling them all this. As if she could read their minds. Bertha responded,

"I am telling you gals this because I want you to know that when you look at another person, don't look at the color of their skin to know them but what's in their heart. Remember I do have a Negro grandmother, but to look at me on the outside you would never think so. I always feel guilty about how dark-skin Negroes are treated—having to work in the cotton fields, going to poor schools, not being paid much for the work they do…living in shacks, I had all the privileges of being white, but deep down I know part of me is a Negro. Remember the man I told you was my father, he owned the cotton gin in Money? Well, he sent me to the best schools, and I wore the best clothes. I was able to live in the biggest house and ate the finest foods. I always had the money I needed to travel to many places. Dark- skinned Negro people made all of these things possible, by picking cotton in the hot sun."

Estella looked into Miss Bertha's eyes, seeing a tear form in the corner of one of her eyes. "I hope you gals will keep the things I told you with you always. I'm gettin' old, and the doctor told me I don't have long to live."

"It's gettin' late, and we got to be gettin' home, Miss Bertha," Ruth said. She was still thinking about Bertha's story.

"Wait," Estella said. "Didn't you say your father owned the cotton gin in Money? What was his name?"

"His name was Joseph Money and the town—Money—was named after him. My name is Bertha Money."

Estella looked at the woman, shocked with her mouth wide open. "You say your daddy is the man Money, Mississippi is named after?" "That's what I said; he took it over from his father after the war." Ruth also had a shocked look on her face. How could this be? She was standing in front of a white woman—or was she a Negro?

And the town the girls were born in was named after this woman's father—Joseph Money.

"I know y'all have to be goin'," Miss Bertha told them. "Please come back to see me anytime." Reaching out to each girl, Miss Bertha gave them a brief hug.

"We will," Estella said, moving toward the front door of the big house. All the way back to the Jessup house, they talked about Miss

136

Bertha and her family. "Do you think Miss Bertha is telling the truth about her family, Ruth?"

"I don't know, but I think so. Why you think she tell us all that, if it wasn't true? I think she wants to help set as much as she could right, before she meets her maker. You think she white or Negro?" Ruth asks.

Estella just shook her head; to her it didn't make a difference.

Ruth added, "I think she's a good person; she really told us a lot of things about herself, her family, and Money." As they neared the Jessup's house; they noticed dozens of fireflies along the road's edge. "We gettin' home just in time; my family would be upset if 'n we had got here any later."

Just then her Aunt stepped from the shadows of the front door, saying, "I was starting to get worried about y'all. Did you have a good time up at that white lady's house?"

"We sho did," Estella replied. "What did y'all talk about?"

"She showed us her big house and some family pictures, Auntie." Ruth was not sure she wanted to tell anyone all the things Miss Bertha had told them.

"Y'all got here just in time for supper," Ruth's Uncle said as he sat down at the head of the kitchen table. "This food, sho do smell good!"

The girls were hungry after their long walk. Ann placed a big helping of potatoes and ham on each plate. After a few minutes, Carl broke the silence of their meal, adding, "I hope this here Depression get over with soon; ain't no work in town. If things don't get better soon, we may have to move back to Money. Back home we can have a garden, and chickens that give us eggs. We can get apples off the trees, go hunting maybe kill a rabbit or two, and if I'm lucky, get a deer. I like to fish and always catch a lot of 'em. Livin' in Money is a lot easier than here in Greenwood."

"Don't feel bad, Carl, about moving back to Money if 'n we have to. Looks to me like everybody's havin' a hard time every since the Depression done come on us. Even the white folks ain't got much money," Ann told him.

CHAPTER 19

PaPa's Lesson

The school year was coming to an end soon; Estella had worked hard, passing all her classes. In just a few days she would graduate. She was expecting her brother to come by and pick her up to go home to prepare for her graduation day.

"I can't wait for Leroy to pick me up, Ruth." "How you know your brother coming?"

"Zac told me when he brought me the food Papa sent me." "I miss my folks and will be glad to see them."

The next morning, just as Zac had promised, Estella woke to the sound of a wagon near the Jessup house. She was praying it was Leroy to take her back home. She pulled back the window curtain next to her bed, her heart racing as she saw the familiar wagon and her brother tying the reins to a tree near the house.

"Yes, it's Leroy!" Estella shouted.

"What's going on?" Ruth asked in a sleepy voice. "Leroy's here to pick me up."

"Why he here so early? He must have left Money before dawn," Ruth mumbled.

"That boy always want to get me out of bed—he thinks it's funny." Estella laughed, but was glad to know they would be back home before lunch. She quickly dressed and washed her hands and face in cold water from the pump in the kitchen. Carl and Ann were still in bed.

"I can fix you some breakfast, Ruth," Estella told her.

"You'll do no such thing, young lady," Ann said, surprising the two girls as she walked into the kitchen. "I do the cooking around here. You go tell that brother of yours he can come in and have some breakfast. Ain't nobody goin' to bite him. I know he must be hungry after that long ride from Money."

As they ate breakfast, they talked about how hard things were getting because of the Depression.

"It's time we be gettin' home; you ready to go, gal? I told Mama we'd be home by lunch time. Thanks for a good breakfast, Miss Ann," Leroy said.

On the way to Money, Estella looked at the passing countryside. Although she had traveled this road many times, it was different this time. She would be the first in her family to graduate from eighth grade. She had a boyfriend and had gone to Big Ben's place; and she'd heard the stories Miss Bertha told her. The Depression was hard on everyone, but so many interesting and good things had happened over the past two years.

"Gal what you thinking about?" Leroy interrupted her train of thought.

"I was thinking about all the things I've done in the last two years."

"It shouldn't take you long!" Leroy said, laughing.

"Boy, don't start that stuff with me," Estella said, slapping Leroy on his back. Then both of them let out a loud laugh.

"You done got a lot more schooling than me, gal—maybe you can teach me something about what you learned in Greenwood."

"You mean you want little ole me to teach you?" They both laughed again. The small mule-drawn wagon pulled into a yard Estella knew well. She was home before she knew it.

Her mother was in the back yard hanging clothes on the line to dry. Looking up to see Estella and Leroy, she ran to Estella, giving her a big hug.

"I missed you!" her mother whispered in her ear. "I missed you too, Mama."

"Glad to see you home!" her Grandfather added, walking over to the wagon, giving her a big hug.

The day was hot, so the family ate lunch in the backyard on a wooden table and benches Paul had built when Estella was only two years old. "You goin' be the first in this family to finish eighth grade," her Grandfather told her with a big smile on his face.

Julia looked at her and pointed her finger, telling her, "Gal, I believe you goin' make somin' of yourself." Leroy sat at the end of the table rolling his eyes.

Paul noticed Leroy. "Boy, why you rolling your eyes like that? You oughts to be glad your sister doin' good in school!" Leroy dropped his head, not wanting to look at Paul.

"We all happy Estella doin' good in school—and that goes for you too, Leroy," Julia told him as she carried the dishes back into the house.

For the next few hours, as the sun began to set in the sky, Paul and Estella sat on the front steps of the small shack, talking about the test she had taken for Mrs. Williams, and the upcoming graduation. "You know when you told me you wanted to go to school in Greenwood, I didn't know how good you would do but, I knew you could do anything you tried to do. You always asking why this and

why that, so I know you needed good schoolin'."

"But Papa, I still don't know why Negroes get treated the way we do."

Paul knew it was time to help his granddaughter learn an important life lesson, he replied, *"I think that's 'cause some people think they better than other people 'cause they skin ain't the same color. Some people make lots of money off working Negroes hard and they pay 'em very little. I know this; the bottom today, goin' be the top tomorrow. You must keep goin' to school; 'cause good schooling can take you places that Negroes ain't ever seen. Remember there is good and bad in all of us—no one is all good or all bad. When you on top, you can always fall; and when you on the bottom, ain't no place to go but up. When you ain't got but a little bit, try to make it go as far as you can; waste not, want not. Always respect other people, even the ones you don't like. Keep your head high even when things ain't goin your way and times be hard. One last thing I'm goin' tell you; love and respect for yourself and others will carry you far."*

Estella smiled at her Grandfather; he was so smart, and she loved him with all her heart. Looking up, she was surprised to see the setting sun. They had talked for a long time. She would always remember all the things her Grandfather had told her.

The next few days, Estella enjoyed being home with her family. "Mama, you know I'm goin' to need a white dress for my graduation."

"I can make you a dress," her mother replied.

"No Mama, my dress has to be just like all the other girls in my class."

"Gal, how much that kind of dress cost?"

"Five dollars Mama." Estella knew that for their family, five dollars was a lot of money.

"But Estella, we ain't got no five dollars. Maybe Papa can help you out."

"I'll ask him when he come back from the woods."

"He ain't got no money since this here Depression; ain't nobody got much of nothing," Leroy added.

That afternoon Estella asked her Grandfather if he could buy her graduation dress. "Gal, I wish I could— but the crop ain't paying much, and the man who owns this here shack, land, and cotton field ain't got much money to pay out. Sharecroppers just got to live off the fat of the land. We better off than most people. We can fish, hunt, and grow our own food in the garden and from fruit trees. We got pigs, cows, and chicken. Folks that live in town ain't got none of that. But ain't nobody got no money—I sure ain't."

Estella knew if she didn't have the right dress, she might be the only one in her class who didn't. She would not feel right, so she would just not walk in with her class. She looked at her Grandfather and mother, not wanting them to feel sad because they couldn't afford her graduation dress. She hugged them both.

"You know it ain't no matter what dress I graduate in long as I graduate," she told them.

"That's a good way to think about it," Paul replied. "I am glad you understand."

"I got me one good daughter," her mother said, looking into Estella's eyes.

"You got a good son, too," Leroy said, not wanting to be left out. "You're a good boy," Paul told him. "Now go out and kill two chickens for supper tonight." Leroy smiled then walked out the back door.

Little Elizabeth, who had just had her tenth birthday, asked, "What about me; ain't I good too?"

Hugging Elizabeth, her mother added, "You good and Laura, too— now, everybody happy?" They all laughed.

"Mattie and Zac goin' to bring their wagon, so we can all go to your graduation together," Julia said. "That way we got three wagons and don't work one or two mules too hard."

Hearing this, Estella knew her graduation was near; she still could not believe tomorrow she would finish eighth grade.

Estella could not sleep—she tossed and turned in and out of sleep, thinking about her graduation. She could not wait to hear the familiar sound of their brown old rooster crowing in the morning, knowing it would be the start of her graduation day.

CHAPTER **20**

Some Kind of Day

Estella's feet hit the floor before the rooster stopped crowing. "Y'all better get up," she called out, waking everyone in the small house. Julia was the first one to come out of her small bedroom, followed by Elizabeth and Laura; as the girls dressed, Estella started breakfast.

"Is that lazy boy still in the bed?" Julia asked.

"You know how that boy likes to hold on to the covers," Paul replied.

"Not today –he ain't goin' to make me late for my graduation!" Estella added, as she walked out the back door and over to the water pump, taking a long-handled dipper that hung from a hook. Filling the dipper with cold water, she walked back to Leroy's bedroom, being careful not to spill a drop. Standing over her brother, she poured the cold water onto his face. She laughed loudly as he jumped up with a startled look on his face.

His eyes were as big as saucers. "Hey, gal—what's wrong with you? You done lost your mind." Estella ran out of the room, laughing.

"I got him up, Mama!"

"I bet you did—that boy still mumbling and fussin'." Julia continued to cook breakfast; like most mornings, the smell of ham and eggs filled the air. Just as the family sat down, there was a knock at the door.

Estella jumped up—expecting it to be Zac. She opened the door to see him standing with a big smile and wink as she motioned him into the house.

"Young man, you always get here when food is on the table," Julia said.

"Yes, Mrs. Reynolds, and it sho look and smell good too!" As Zac took a seat at the table, the family could hear another sound outside. Once again, Estella ran to the door; opening the door she quickly stepped out to see Mattie and her husband, Joseph, walking toward the porch steps.

Mattie was dressed in a pretty red dress with a big pink flower in her hair, and Joseph had on his best black, church suit. At six-foot-five he was tall, dark, and good looking. He always told people most folks had to look up to him. Zac, Mattie, and Joseph waited in the front room as the rest of the family prepared for the trip to Greenwood and the graduation ceremony.

Paul was the first to be ready; he came out from a small room at the back of the house, dressed in a dark blue suit and black shoes that he wore only to church and special occasions. His pocket watch tucked into his suit pocket with its gold chain hanging down. Soon Julia entered the front room; she wore a light-blue dress and big blue hat with a white flower she had picked from her garden the day before.

"You look great, Mrs. Reynolds," Zac said, as she entered the room.

"Thank you, Zac."

Estella came out of her room dressed in a white dress she had worn to church many times. "That dress looks good on you," her Grandfather told her.

"Oh Papa, you done seen this here dress at church lots of times." "It looks better on you today."

"You just want to make me feel good," Estella told him.

"Where's Leroy," her mother asked.

"That boy better not be trying to make me late," Estella added with a big frown on her face.

Her brother shouted back, "I ain't trying to make you late. I was just helping Elizabeth tie her shoes. Laura wanted me to help her too."

"Well, I hope y'all ready, 'cause'n we need to be gettin' on our way. The graduation ain't goin' to wait for us!"

The family walked out of the house across the small front yard toward the three mule-drawn wagons that awaited them. Zac and Estella were in the lead wagon, with Paul, Julia, and Elizabeth in the second wagon, and Joseph, Mattie, Leroy, and Laura riding behind them. Forming a small caravan, the three wagons started down the narrow dirt road to Greenwood.

She could not stop thinking about their destination—today was her eighth grade graduation. She couldn't wait, but she would have to, because mule-drawn wagons did not move fast…it looked to her that the wagons were moving slower than ever. For the next hour, she and Zac talked about Money and their life in Mississippi.

"I wants to go North, Zac, when I get enough money. The South is always goin be like this, and it ain't no place for me. What you goin' do Zac? You gonna stay here in the South, or go North too?"

Zac didn't answer; instead, he was looking down the road to see several horses off in the distance. "Some people coming this way on horses," Zac said, looking far down the road. The wagons and men on horseback grew closer. The man on the lead horse put his hands into the air just in front of the caravan of wagons; it was the Sheriff, followed by four deputies.

"Where you folks goin' on this fine day," the Sheriff asked Zac. "We on our way to my graduation," Estella answered.

"Well, now—you must be one smart nigger," the Sheriff said, with a smirk on his face. Zac remembered he had some moonshine under the covers in the back of the wagon; he hoped the Sheriff didn't start snooping around too much. Paul had gotten down from his wagon; he walked up to the Sheriff, asking him if he could help him.

"No, boy—ain't nothin' you can do to help me. Less'n you have done seed the boy we looking for…the nigger who done beat up a white man just outside Greenwood. If we find him before the mob, we goin' to put him in jail. If that mob finds him first, they are goin' to string him up. Did y'all see him walking down this road?"

"We ain't seed nobody," Paul said loudly.

"I need to take a look in y'all wagons," the Sheriff told Paul, who was now walking back to his wagon.

"Help yourself," Paul called back to him. The Sheriff nodded his head toward his deputies. Three deputies dismounted; Zac became very nervous as one of the deputies approached the wagon he and Estella were riding. As the Sheriff reached the back of the wagon, something moved deep in the woods behind them. Seeing the movement, the Sheriff and his men quickly remounted their horses and rode off down the road toward the woods.

"Thank God they gone," Julia told Zac.

"If that Sheriff had found my moonshine, bad things could have happened to me," Zac told them.

"Why you selling moonshine, anyway," Estella asked.

"I told you I ain't never goin' to make big money picking cotton. Since this here Depression, I make more money than I ever made, by selling moonshine."

Estella knew Zac was right. Suddenly she recognized very familiar houses; looking ahead, her schoolhouse was just minutes away.

"I think lot of folks here for this graduation," Julia said, seeing about fifteen wagons in front of the school house. Estella, so excited and full of joy, did not wait for Zac to help her down from the wagon. She quickly jumped to the ground when the wagon stopped.

The rest of her family climbed down from the wagons and walked into the school.

Estella noticed many of her classmates were already in the room that was typically used for lunch and a study area. It was also used for punishment when someone got out of line and had to stay after school. Today there would be no punishment—only joy, happiness, and fun. The room was filled with students, teachers, friends, and families.

The first person she saw, as they entered the room was Tom, the boy she had the fight with during her first weeks of school; it seemed like so long ago, and now it was her last day at this school. Before the graduation ceremony, Estella walked around the room introducing her family to her classmates and teachers. When Mrs. Williams entered the room, Estella motioned for her family to come and meet her.

"Mrs. Williams, this here is my mama and Grandfather; my brother, Leroy; my sisters Elizabeth and Laura; my Aunt and Uncle;

and Zac, my boyfriend. Y'all, this here is Mrs. Williams; you always hear me talking 'bout. She is our headmistress."

Julia was as shocked as Estella had been to see a well- dressed Negro woman as headmistress.

"My granddaughter has told us a lot about you," Paul said, shaking Mrs. Williams' hand.

"She say you one smart lady," Leroy added.

"Thank you; it is very nice to meet Estella's family. Excuse me, but it's time we get started."

Mrs. Williams turned and walked to the front of the room. "Please be seated!" she shouted. The room had been noisy with people talking; now it became quiet as people took their seats to hear Mrs. Williams' commencement speech. You could hear a pin drop.

"Welcome, all of you. This is a great day—a day that until recently was not possible because just sixty-eight years ago, we Negroes became free to go to school, to live and work as free people.

Just sixty-eight years ago, the Civil War came to an end after Abraham Lincoln freed the slaves. In this room, some of our grandparents were slaves. Today they are proud of you because you know how to read, write, do arithmetic, and know how to use good English. You are graduating eighth grade, something none of your grandparents and few of your parents have been able to do. Remember as you move on with your life to always respect everyone, because everyone wants to be respected. Respect others even when they don't respect you. Don't do something to others you would not want done to you. Be proud of yourselves, but remember you did not get here by yourselves. Always keep your heads high even when others try to make you put it down. Learn as much as you can all of your life. Give love to others, even when they don't show you love. Last but not least, remember skin color is on the outside and tells one nothing about what's on the inside. I am very proud of each and every one of you— now go out and show the world who you are."

The whole room erupted with loud applause that went on and on. Estella thought that much of what Mrs. Williams was saying sounded much like what her mother and grandpa taught her. Always help others; you know how to read and write, and if you know someone who can't, then help them to learn. The applause stopped when Mrs. Williams put her arms into the air, saying, "Thank you, thank you." At last the room became quiet once more.

"Will the candidates for graduation please stand? When I call your name, please come to the front of the room to receive your diploma."

"Ann Smith." Each student walked to the front of the room to receive the diploma they had worked so hard for. "Estella Reynolds." As her name was called, this was what the young girl had dreamed about for as long as she could remember. How she got in front of Mrs. Williams, she didn't know—she must have been walking on air. Mrs. Williams handed her the piece of paper she had worked so hard for. Walking back to her seat, she saw tears of joy rolling down her mother's face, and her grandpa had the biggest smile she had ever seen on his face. Even Leroy had a little tear in the corner of his eye. Estella took her seat just as Ruth Jessup got up to receive her diploma, and now it was Estella who shed tears. Estella noticed that not all the girls in her class had on the same white dresses; besides her, two others did not have the same white dress for their graduation. Finally, Mrs. Williams called the last name, and the graduation was over. To Estella it was over much too fast—it had taken so long to get here, and it was over much too quick.

She had done it—she had finished the eighth grade. People were now standing around shaking hands, hugging and patting the students on the back. Mrs. Williams came over to talk to Julia and Paul. "Estella has been one good student all year; she's told me a lot about you two and her boyfriend. She thinks the world of her family." Mrs. Williams stepped away to talk to other families. Leroy looked at Estella, saying, "You think you a big shot now," then let out a big laugh. Julia poked Leroy with a finger. "Leave that gal alone, and let her enjoy herself." Little Elizabeth, wanting to be like her big sister, just stood next to her, looking up at her.

"We got it," Ruth shouted, proudly waving her diploma above her head.

"We sure did—and I wish we could be this happy every day," Estella replied, hugging Ruth. Just then she was surprised to see a familiar face over Ruth's shoulder. It was Miss Bertha. "Look who here, Ruth!" Estella pointed over her shoulder. Ruth turned to see what Estella was talking about. The two girls walked over to where Miss Bertha was standing.

"We glad to see you here," Ruth said.

"I wouldn't miss this for the world," Miss Bertha replied, walking back to where their families had gathered. Estella introduced Miss Bertha to her family, and then Ruth did the same.

Once again, the sound of Mrs. Williams' voice cut thru the hot spring air of the room. "May I have your attention?" The room became quiet once more. "On the table at the back of this room are gifts that have been left by friends and family of our graduates. I will be passing them out. When I call your name, please come forward to receive your gift."

Mrs. Williams read the name on each gift, as each student came forward. Estella did not expect a gift, since she knew her folks had no money for gifts. When all the names had been called she knew she wouldn't get a gift and started to move away from the table. "Wait—I have missed one gift," Mrs. Williams called, "Estella Reynolds."

She couldn't believe her ears—*who had left a gift for her,* she wondered? Taking the small package from Mrs. Williams, with her hands shaking, she tore open the thin blue paper to find a beautiful silk and lace white handkerchief inside. She had never seen lace on a handkerchief. Tears welled in her eyes—this was the best day of her life. Who had given her such a nice present? This kind of handkerchief must have cost a lot. Had Zac saved up for it?

Looking at her family and Zac, she asked, "Who gave me this?" She held up the lace handkerchief. But no one stepped forward. She walked over to Mrs. Williams to ask the same question; but Mrs. Williams shook her head.

"Did you like my gift," a voice behind her asked—it was Miss Bertha.

Holding the handkerchief out before her, Estella asked, "You gave me this, Miss Bertha?"

"Yes. I wanted to make sure you got something nice for all your hard work." Estella lunged toward Bertha, hugging her so hard that the woman could hardly breathe.

With tears rolling down her cheek, Estella whispered, "This is the best thing anyone ever gave me!"

"Did you look under the handkerchief?"

"No, ma'am." Estella had been so excited; she didn't realize there was something else inside the blue wrapping paper. She gently unrolled the paper, wondering what it could be. And suddenly, a twenty dollar bill popped out from under the paper. Twenty dollars was more money than Estella had ever had at one time; she could do so much with this money. She had saved about six dollars in a little tin box she placed in a hole at the base of a tree behind her house. She was saving every penny she found, earned, or had been given since she was eight. She knew that one day the saved money would come in handy; she just knew it would—but for what, she didn't know.

In only an hour or more, the graduation room was almost empty. Only a few people stood around. "I think it's time we be gettin' on," her Grandfather said.

"Good idea," Julia replied. "We want to be home before dark. I don't like being on the road at night."

Roscoe Jessup came up to them just as the family started for the wagon. "We goin' follow y'all back to Money so we can take Ruth home."

As the families walked back to their wagons, a gentle wind was blowing, helping to keep the heat from being unbearable. The four wagons carrying the families moved slowly down the hot dusty road. This time, Paul drove the lead wagon as the others followed. The sun had just started to set when Estella notice something funny in a tree up the road a bit.

"What that, Zac?"

"I don't know," Zac answered." As the wagon moved slowly toward the tree, he realized it was something horrible. It was a man hanging from a rope, his head bent down and his arms hanging limp at his sides. All four wagons came to a sudden stop, as everyone gazed at the horrible sight before them. "Oh my God," Julia screamed.

"Oh no," Estella called out, "Not today—not this day of all days!"

"When will this stop," Zac asked. "I'm goin' to cut him down!"
"No, Zac!" Paul shouted, motioning for Zac to stay seated. "If you cut him down, the wild animals goin' to get him; just let him be. Let somebody else cut him down. We better be gettin' on now; the children and women don't need to look at this too long."

"Dat must be that boy the Sheriff and his boys were looking for," Zac said, as the four wagons pulled away.

But all Estella could think of was how the day had started with such joy—and now this, the worst thing she had ever seen, besides her Aunt being shot. "I hope people can stop doin' things like this to other people."

"Maybe one day they will; it ain't goin be soon enough for me," Julia said, with tears rolling down her face. "I hope white folks stop doin' that to our people one day. We all people, just like they is!"

As they continued back to Money, everyone talked about the joy and sadness of the day. Estella knew the moment she looked up in that tree and saw a young Negro man, who could have been Zac, that she would never be happy in the South. Negroes could not drink from the same water fountains as whites. Negroes always had to step aside to let whites by. In the South, Negroes worked in the hot sun all day and got little pay, and always had to say yes sir and no sir, yes ma'am and no ma'am to white folks. Worst of all, in the South, Negroes could be hung for getting out of place. To her, this was a place to leave, not stay.

"I got to get out of the South, Zac! This ain't no place for me!"
"Where are you goin'." Zac asked, with a funny look on his face.
"North...maybe Chicago. I got an Uncle there. I'm going to take the train, when I gets enough money to buy a ticket."

"I wish I could go with you. I was thinking on gettin' out of here myself. But I got to take care of my father."

The sun was setting when the four wagons pulled into the Reynolds family's front yard. "It feels good to be home," Julia said, as she and Estella climbed down from the wagon, with Leroy's help. "This has been some kind of day," she added.

Estella waved to Zac and the Jessups as they continued down the road. Following Leroy, she pushed at his back, knowing he would fuss. "It's too late for supper now, boy. Guess you be going to bed hungry!"

"That's what you say, gal! I know Mama made an apple pie before we left and it's sitting over yonder in that window."

"Boy, you always keep up with some food," Paul said.

"Mama, can't we cut that pie? I'm hungry, and it's gettin' late."
"I guess so; bring it over here so I can do the cutting,"

"Cut me a big piece," Leroy told her; handing over the pie.

"We all have to get a little of this pie, and you goin get the same size piece as the rest of us."

"If anybody gets a big piece, it sure be me! It was me that graduated today!"

"She right," Paul said. "Now y'all stop that fuss!"

The family sat on the porch, eating the pie and talking about the graduation. Paul and Julia told Estella how proud they were of her one more time before they all went to bed.

Estella did not sleep well the night of her graduation; she had seen and done so much. She decided to repay her family by making breakfast. It was her way of saying thank you. The next day she tried not to make much noise, but the smell of food cooking must have woken them anyway. Soon she heard footsteps and voices, as one by one they got out of bed.

"Good morning," Julia said as she entered the kitchen. "You got the house smelling like bacon and pancakes this morning. Why you up so early, girl?"

"I had a hard time sleeping. I was thinkin' 'bout yesterday. It was the best day of my life, and one of the worst."

"I know—seeing that poor man hanging in that tree...ain't nobody supposed to see a thing like what we saw! Try not to think about it," she added, hugging her daughter.

"What's burning," Leroy asked, coming out of his bedroom. "Don't you worry, Leroy...I almost burned the bacon." Estella scolded him.

"One of these days, she gonna burn this place down," Leroy said, laughing, as he walked out the back door to wash his face with the cold water he pumped from the well.

CHAPTER 21

Fishing and Celebrating

It was already two months since her graduation, and Estella was helping her mother wash down the front porch. As she pumped water into the bucket, she was thinking how nice it would be to go to the lake instead of mopping the front porch. Just then a voice said, "How about we go fishin' gal?"

Turning around, she was surprised to see Zac standing behind her, holding a bucket in one hand and small shovel in the other. "Well, what you say? You wanna go to catch some fish?"

"I don't know; I supposed to stay here and help Mama around the house—we got to mop the front porch, wash Papa's overalls, and see bout the garden."

Overhearing Zac and Estella, Julia said, "Y'all go ahead and have fun."

"But Mama, you got so much work to do, and I need to help you around here."

"Gal, that boy says he wants to take you fishin', so stop fussing and go catch some fish."

Leroy, who had come in from picking apples to be canned, added, "You go fish! I bet I will get most of your work round here."

"Boy... you ain't goin' to be overworked, so you just leave your sister alone. I'll make Laura and Elizabeth help."

"Zac, I need to finish the dishes before we go." "That be fine, gal. I can go dig some worms."

After warming the dishwater on the stove and washing all the breakfast dishes, Estella walked to the back yard, where Zac was digging for worms. Looking over at Zac, she asked, "Ain't you got enough worms by now?"

"Yes, I got plenty of bait. We can go now."

Zac placed the bait bucket and shovel next to the long cane poles and large fish bucket in the back of the wagon. He easily jumped into the seat, leaning down for Estella, pulling her up next to him. No sooner had the wagon started to move than he leaned over and gave Estella a long passionate kiss. Estella looked into his eyes, and the feeling she always got came rushing over her once more.

"Zac you shouldn't be kissing me like that, so near my house." "Why? Your folks know how I feel about you, gal!" All the way to the lake they hugged and kissed.

"We're here," Zac said, when the blue waters of the lake came into view. It was a small lake set back in the woods; only a few people ever came here to fish. "We done picked a good day to fish—ain't no wind or waves, and the lake is still. I think we goin' be catching some fish here. I fixed this pole for you; all you got to do is put a worm on the hook. You know how to fish, gal?"

"Sho, I know how to fish—I go with my grandpa and brother sometime."

"That's good, we can go right at it and I won't need to show you how," Zac said.

As they both cast their fishing lines into the nearly still water, the minute Estella's line hit the water, her cork started to move up and down. "I got a bite," Estella called out. She pulled her line in, and at the end of her line was a little sun fish.

"That fish ain't big enough to bite," Zac said laughing.

Estella took the small fish off the hook, being careful not to kill it. As she gently placed the small fish back into the water, she noticed Zac's cork go under the water. "Look, Zac—you got one too!" Zac shouted, "I got a big one!" He pulled back on his pole and slowly pulled a very big fish from the water. "Now that's what I call a fish!"

"That's a good looking fish Zac!"

As Estella turned back to watch her cork, she saw it go under the water. She quickly pulled back on her line, but it would not move. "This must be a big one too—come help me bring it in Zac!"

Zac dropped his pole and took hold of her pole. "I don't know what you done got hold to gal! But it ain't moved for a while." Zac pulled on her line; at last, the biggest catfish Estella had ever seen came out of the water and landed at her feet.

"Now that's what I call a fish! It is bigger than any fish I seen," she laughed and pointed to her catch.

"That be one big catfish—gotta be more than six pounds!"

Zac looked down at the water's edge, and picked-up the biggest, meanest-looking catfish from the water's edge. She watched as he unhooked the fish from her line; the big fish jumped from his strong hands, trying to get back into the water. Finally he was able stop the fish with his foot, placing one foot on its tail, and quickly put the big fish into their bucket. Over the next two hours, they enjoyed talking and catching another fifteen good-sized fish…but none as big as Estella's catfish.

"I think it's about time we be gettin' on back home, gal."

"Yes, we done caught half the fish—in this lake!" They both laughed as they walked back to the wagon. "I done had me some fun fishing, Zac," Estella said.

"Me too, gal! Next time; I will catch the biggest fish. But we needs to get home, befo' these fish spoil; it is still too hot for them to set too long." Zac placed the fishing poles and bucket in the back of the wagon, pulled Estella up on the seat next to him, and tapped the mule with the reins—and down the road they went.

"Look," Estella called out, as they neared her house. "What all them wagons doin' at my house?"

"I don't know—guess we just got to go and find out," Zac said. "I hope nothing bad done happened," she replied, jumping down from the wagon and almost running toward the house. She opened the door and a loud sound came rushing at her, "Surprise!"

Estella saw the faces of everyone she knew: her mother and Grandfather, brother, sisters, aunts, Uncles, friends—some she hadn't seen for months—and even Mrs. Williams. So many people had come to celebrate her accomplishment of being the first in her family to graduate eighth grade.

"We goin' give you a big party for your graduation," her mother shouted loudly.

She didn't know what to think. "Zac, you knew 'bout this all the time?"

"I kinda did, "he replied, and the whole group erupted in laughter. "You just go get washed up so we can get this party going," her Grandfather told her.

Zac and Estella moved through the crowded house and into the back yard to wash up. Once in the back yard, they could not believe what they saw: a long table made from leftover lumber from the chicken coop and wooden boxes from the barn. The table was covered with white tablecloths borrowed from several neighbors and family members—and the chairs she recognized from other houses. The table was full of food of all kinds: fried chicken, turkey, ham, greens, potato salad, black-eyed peas, pies of all kinds, buckets of lemonade, and a cake with a cardboard and paper graduation cap cut out of a newspaper in the center.

Everyone waited for Estella to take a seat at the bountiful table before sitting down. Reverend Lockwood stood up and gave one of his long prayers. The table buzzed with talk about how glad everyone was that Ruth and Estella were some of the first Negroes from Money to finish the eighth grade.

Paul talked about Estella being a little girl and how she would always ask—why this and why that. Her mother added that she had always been a hard worker and good helper. Leroy talked about how she had always teased him and tried to beat him at everything.

Going around the tables, one by one her family and friends testified about Estella's strong character, determined mind, and kindness. The last person to speak was Mrs. Williams. "I knew Estella was so smart and willing to do the work and study hard. That's how she was able to skip two grades."

And with that, the group erupted with clapping hands and shouts of praise. Estella knew she had done well, and she was on top of the world this afternoon. Even the weather smiled upon her—the wind was light, and the air was just warm enough.

Reverend Lockwood rose and asked Estella to say a few words. Estella stood and started to speak, standing behind her chair. "I just want to say thank you—thank you to each and every one of y'all. My papa told me I could do anything I put my mind to, and my mama is always here for me no matter what. My brother and little sisters made things fun, and sometimes made me mad." Laughter could be heard all around the table. "My Aunts and Uncles, my friends always be here for me when I need them. And my boyfriend Zac is fun to be around—he made lots of trips to Greenwood to pick me up, and he just took me fishing today. My teachers and Mrs. Williams helped with my schooling in Greenwood. I could not have graduated without them. Y'all helped me in so many ways; I love you all so much! I guess this is a good time to tell you that when I get enough money, I want to go to Chicago. So I can make more money by gettin' a good job in Chicago."

Julia and Paul were shocked to hear that Estella still wanted to go North to Chicago; she hadn't mentioned it to them for some time.

Estella sat down after she spoke; the crowd of family members and friends were also surprised to hear her plans to leave Money.

"Can we eat now?" Leroy asked, breaking the silence, rubbing his belly and rolling his eyes.

"Boy, you always ready to eat," Julia told him. Everyone started to laugh. "The food ain't goin run away!"

Over nearly two hours, the group enjoyed the food and conversation. As the sun started to set behind the trees, the mosquitoes and other bugs started to bite. One by one the guests started to leave, taking tablecloths and chairs with them. The party was over, but everyone had a great time. Estella's family started to clear the tables, able to see by the full moon above them.

CHAPTER **22**

A Letter to Uncle

The next day Estella was back in the cotton fields. It reinforced the reason she wanted to move North to Chicago; she hated being in the fields and working in the hot sun. She hated getting her hands and arms stuck with cotton buds and sometimes bleeding. Most of all, she hated that all she saw were Negroes in the fields, being paid very little for the hard, rough work they all did. She knew this was not what she wanted to do much longer. The day she left the South would be the day she would look forward to, as long as she was in Money.

The first day back in the cotton fields had been long and hot, but at last it was over. Walking home that evening, she decided to write her Uncle Leamon up North in Chicago. After dinner that night Estella asked her mother if she had Leamon's address in Chicago.

"I think so," Julia replied. "I'll look for it. What you want it for?"
"I want to write him and ask if I can come to Chicago and can he takes me in for a while."

"Gal, you ain't got no money to go to no Chicago—and besides, we need you here to help get in the cotton."

"Don't worry, Mama; I ain't goin' nowhere till we get in the cotton, and I get the money I need."

Julia left the room, and after a little while came back carrying a white envelope. "Your Uncle's address is on this here envelope," handing the envelope to her daughter.

"Thanks, Mama. You know how much I love my family; this be a hard thing to do—but I just need to do it. Don't worry 'bout giving me no money. I've been saving up."

"Gal, I know if 'n you want to do something, you always find a way to do it," her mother told her, petting her head. Estella sat down and started to write to her Uncle.

Dear Uncle Leamon,

I hope you are doin' all right in Chicago. I just finished eighth grade. I want to come to Chicago to get a good job and get out of the cotton fields. I hope you can take me in for a while until I can find work. I hope this here Depression will be over by the time I come North.

I am working in the fields and will do whatever work I can to save enough money for the train ticket. This will take some time to do. I will write you again, when I got the money to come North. Please write me back soon, to let me know if you can take me in for a while.

Love—your niece, Estella Reynolds.

Estella looked at the letter she had just worked on. It was the first time she had used her schooling to write anyone. The next day as she placed the letter in the mailbox, she realized this could be the first step on her road from Money. The day after she wrote the letter to her Uncle, her Aunt Mattie stopped by as she sometimes did.

"I got some work over in Greenwood, how about you come with me, Estella? This rich white lady wants me to come three days a week to help her maid do some cleaning. You said at your party you wanted to go up North to Chicago. I know this lady got lots of work—she told me if I could find somebody to help me she would pay them too. Do you want the work, gal?"

Estella was overjoyed—this could be what she needed to give her enough money to buy her ticket to Chicago. "How much this work paying?" Estella asked with a smile on her face.

"She says she goin' pay me a dollar for three days. If we do good work, she may give us a little extra. The only thing is we got to stay two nights in Greenwood when we do this work. The lady said she got a room at the back of the house where we can sleep."

"That's okay with me, 'cause it be a lot more money than I gets in the cotton field."

"Well then, I'm glad you want to come with me. We got to be there Monday, and we can come back to Greenwood Wednesday after work."

"What y'all talkin' 'bout?" Julia asked, upon entering the house through the back door.

"Mama, Aunt Mattie just told me she got some work for me over in Greenwood. Can I go with her? We will help clean this white lady's house, and she got a room to stay. I will be back here on Wednesdays. Okay, Mama?"

"Gal, if'n you can make money in this Depression—do it!"

That night Zac, the Reverend and Mrs. Lockwood, Mattie, and the Jessups all came to supper. Each week the neighbors would host a community dinner; in tough times. What one family didn't have to eat, another family would.

The prayer was said by Reverend Lockwood. "Can you pass the chicken, please?" Leroy asked.

"I know you want to get your hands on that chicken before I did," Estella told him.

"Don't you two start!" Julia said, looking over at Estella. Mattie laughed, "Those two always at each other."

"They just being brother and sister," Reverend Lockwood added. "What's this I hear about you goin' to Greenwood to work with Mattie?" Paul asked Estella.

"Papa, I'm goin' get paid lot more money helping Mattie than I will working in the field. I think I can make enough to buy my ticket to go up North."

"We can talk about it later," Paul replied, with a small frown.

The family and friends enjoyed a great supper. The talk around the table was about how bad things were since the Depression started.

"You think Roosevelt goin' to get things back on track?" Carl Jessup asked.

"I don't know, but he sho trying," Paul told him.

"Things look to me like they ain't gettin' no better," Carl replied. "I see lot of white folks having a hard time just like us," the reverend added.

"President Roosevelt got his hands full. Some folks say we may get into another war."

Reverend Lockwood pointed a finger toward the ceiling, saying, "It's all in God's hands, and ain't much we can do about it."

Zac had been quiet until now, finally saying, "When things get to the bottom, ain't nowhere to go but up."

"You sho got that right," Paul responded.

"Time sho goes by fast," Ann Jessup said. "I think we better be gettin' on down the road toward home."

"I think I'll be goin' too," Zac said.

Soon only Mattie, Joseph, and Estella remained around the table. "Mattie, what you and Estella up to," Paul asked, as he walked back toward them.

"I got some work over in Greenwood, and I want Estella to help me. You know the family I used to work for asked me 'bout working for this rich family over in Greenwood, 'cause they ain't got enough money to keep me on with the Depression and all."

Paul rolled his eyes. "They goin' to pay good?"

"Yes, they rich and goin pay us more than we could make working in the fields."

"Sound good to me," Paul said, looking at Estella and Julia. "Oh, thank you, Papa," Estella cried out, giving her Grandfather a big hug.

"We goin' to Greenwood in the morning. We be back on Wednesday night. The family got a room where we can sleep."

"I'll be ready in the morning, Aunt Mattie."

"I'll be back here bright and early. Be sho you be ready," Mattie said.

CHAPTER **23**

Estella's New Work

E stella woke early the next morning, excited to know she would be going to Greenwood with her Aunt Mattie to see about work. Dressing quickly, she washed her face and grabbed an apple from the kitchen table, taking a seat on the porch steps facing the road. It was early; the sun was just breaking through the trees, lighting the road in front of her little shack of a house. As she ate the apple, she wondered about the house and who they would see in Greenwood. Suddenly, she heard a wagon coming. Looking up she saw her Aunt Mattie waving to her.

"You ready, gal?" Mattie asked, motioning for her niece to climb aboard next to her.

"I sho am!" Estella said, as she stepped up on the wagon.

Her Aunt was one of few women she knew that could take the reins of a wagon and manage a mule as well as any man. Estella always admired her Aunt Mattie; she was a strong, hard-working woman. She always stood her ground, with white people and Negroes alike. On the way to Greenwood, they talked about their new work and the family hiring them. Arriving in Greenwood, Mattie took a map from her dress pocket. "They say this place is on the other side of Greenwood."

"Are we lost?"

"This here look like the road where we should turn—don't worry," her Aunt said, laughing, handing her the map.

Estella pointed to the map, saying, "No it ain't! This here map shows a T-shaped road; we is looking fo' one that makes an L shape. Look that must be it up the road a bit."

"You right, gal! You pretty smart!" Mattie said, looking up the road. Turning onto the road, they saw only fields, trees, and some cows. "Maybe this here ain't the right road after all...let's keep goin' for a spell longer Estella said looking over at Mattie."

Suddenly, Estella noticed a big white house about fifty yards down the road. As the house grew nearer, they could see just how big the house was: it had four big white columns in front and a long porch that circled both the ground floor and the second floor. She knew the owners must be rich, because a T Model Ford was parked near the front entrance—a rare sight in Greenwood.

"This got to be the place, Auntie!"

"If 'n this ain't, somebody got lots of money that lives here," Mattie said.

The front door opened and a short Negro woman came out; she was dressed in a maid's uniform. "Y'all must be the help Ms. Brold been looking for."

"We is," Mattie said, getting down from the wagon, with Estella following her.

"Come in. I'll tell Ms. Brold y'all here; wait here." The maid walked down the long hall across from the front door.

"Auntie—this here house is even bigger than Ms. Bertha's house."

"Who is Ms. Bertha?"

"You met her at my graduation."

"Yes, I remember…that white lady—the one you said was really a Negro. But if she got a house almost big as this house? She can't be no Negro," Mattie mumbled; Estella just rolled her eyes.

"Mrs. Brold will see y'all now," the maid told them, re-entering the room. "Come with me. My name is Pat, by the way. What's y'all name?"

"My name is Mattie and this here is my niece Estella."

Entering the next room Estella and Mattie saw two children: a girl who looked to be about ten, and a boy who looked to be fifteen or sixteen. Pat introduced the two children. "This Master Peter and Miss Sue Ann."

A side door of the room opened, and a well-dressed woman who looked to be about fifty entered the room. She was tall for a woman, with deep blue eyes and coal-black hair. Estella thought she looked like one of the ladies in the magazines or movies.

"My name is Mrs. Brold. You must be the help I have been waiting to see. Betsy said you do good work."

"Yes ma'am, we do," Mattie said confidently.

"Well then; I will pay each of you a dollar a day. Is that okay with you both?"

"Yes ma'am!" Mattie said, almost too loudly. It was more money than she had ever been paid in her life for a day's work; Estella couldn't believe her ears.

"Pat, can you show them around now?" Mrs. Brold asked, as she turned and left the room. Pat nodded and led them from room to room, telling them what Mrs. Brold expected them to do. Then they went outside to see the grounds and garden.

"Y'all will be taking care of the garden, and doin' the cooking and the cleaning. I will be goin' to work for two days a week at the Walkers' place. They done come on hard times, with this Depression and all," Pat said, shaking her head slowly. "Mrs. Brold is sending me over to the Walkers for two days a week—that's why she needs y'all here."

Next, she led them down a path behind the garden where a big white coach house stood. It had two large doors in the front and a second floor with windows on each side of the door that lead to a small front porch. The coach house seemed to be very well-kept. Estella noticed a small garden off to one side of the structure. Pat pointed to the small garden, which was in full bloom. "That's my little plot," Pat said proudly. "Y'all can help me eat some of them greens."

"I think you goin' need more help than us to eat all of them greens!" Estella said, laughing.

The three women entered the coach house with Pat leading the way. Inside Mattie and Estella saw a narrow staircase that led to the upper floor. Once at the top of the stairs, Pat showed the two women two small rooms. "This where y'all goin' be sharing," Pat said as she walked into a room that had one small bed.

"That bed ain't big enough for no two folks, less they babies," Mattie said.

"Well then, one of y'all goin have to sleep on the floor." Estella looked at her Aunt with a big frown on her face. Mattie knew she did not like the idea of sleeping on the floor.

"Mrs. Brold said y'all can start work next week. That is, if'n y'all want the work." Pat said, looking at Mattie and Estella with a big smile on her face.

"Next week? I thought we goin' start today," Mattie said.

"The Walkers goin' out of town; so Mrs. Brold want y'all back here Monday before noon."

"We'll be here!" Mattie said, as they walked down the front porch steps toward their wagon. Climbing up to the wagon seat, they both turned to wave at Pat as the wagon turned the corner toward Greenwood.

"What we goin' do now?" Estella asked.

"I got a notion to stop by the Jessups' before we start back to Money."

"That sound good to me, Auntie."

As they continued toward the Jessup house, Estella noticed that since the Depression, she didn't see as many wagons or cars on the road. Most people had no work and many had lost money when the banks had what her Papa called "a run on the banks." He also told her that something called the stock market made lots of white people lose money. Estella did not understand all of that, but she knew it didn't sound good.

Estella and Mattie arrived at the Jessup home about noon, and knocked on their front door. Ann opened the door, surprised to see two very familiar faces. "We didn't know y'all were coming."

"We didn't know we were coming either, Ann; we was at Mrs. Brold's house. We gonna work for her starting Monday."

"That's wonderful! Let me get y'all something to eat. I got some ham, and y'all can have some of this here soup I fixed."

"That's nice of you," Estella said, as she and Mattie sat down at the kitchen table.

"Now y'all have a seat and I'll bring the food." "What kind of work y'all done found?" Carl asked.

"We goin' be working up the road a spell taking care of some white folks' house three days a week."

"Y'all done found work when there ain't no work! That's good—real good," Carl said placing his left hand to his chin.

"God's good, Carl," Mattie replied.

"Why don't you and Estella stay here with us when you in town?" "That sound like a good idea. That way, my niece don't have to sleep on the floor." Mattie laughed, winking at Estella.

"From what y'all tell...the house is just across town, and won't take long to get there from here. What folks back in Money doin'?" Carl asked.

"The same old thing— picking cotton, growing their gardens, fishing, canning, hunting…just trying to get through these hard times," Mattie replied.

"Yes, times are hard for everybody; even the rich white folks done fell on bad times," Ann said.

Estella listened for a while; then she started to talk about her plans to go up North to Chicago. "I hope this new work last long enough to give me the money I need for a ticket and to live on for a while." Estella looked into the next room. Seeing the big radio, she asked, "Do that radio work, Carl?"

"It sho do," he replied, walking over to the big wooden box, and reaching over to turn the dials. As if by magic, the small house filled with the sound of music.

"That be Fred Astaire, Mattie. I loves that song—'Cheek to Cheek'!" Carl said. He turned the dial again, and Estella heard another band. Ann said it was the Dorsey orchestra playing "The Lullaby of Broadway." Estella could not believe that all of this was coming from this thing they called a radio. She had heard a radio from time to time when she came to Greenwood from Money, but she could never just stop and listen. Mattie stared at the radio too, as if she could see the people, bands, and places inside. "Y'all must be the only Negroes that got a radio," Estella said, looking over at Carl and Ann.

"If'n that old man Gray didn't give it to me, we wouldn't have one either," Carl replied, as he turned the dial one more time. Suddenly a man was speaking—he was talking about the latest news.

"Now the headline news, brought to you by NeHi Drink in all the popular flavors. The dust storms in the Great Plains show no signs of letting up. Dust, dust and more dust; the weather man is no help...he says he sees no rain in sight. In other news, the U.S. Congress accepts President Roosevelt's New Deal, the program aimed at easing the Depression."

Estella sat listening to every word; the man giving the news on the radio seemed magical, and the radio was a magic box. A whole world of new people, places, and things opened up as she listened. The others in the house seemed to disappear—it was as if only she and the radio were in the house. She continued to listen and learn about the world of sports, where James Bradock defeated Max Baer in fifteen rounds for the world heavyweight boxing title.

"Having a radio is wonderful," Mattie said. Estella was brought back into the conversation.

"A radio wouldn't do us no good in Money—we ain't got no electricity in our walls," Estella explained. They all laughed.

"I guess you right—a radio and no electric ain't of no use!" Carl said as he turned off the radio.

"What you goin' do, Mattie? You gonna stay with us, or at that white folks' place?"

"I don't know—we got to think on it; but tonight, we best be gettin' back home," Mattie replied.

"Why don't y'all stay the night and get a fresh start in the morning Ann said?"

"That sound good, Ann. I wants to listen to the radio some more."

"I recon ain't nobody back in Money goin miss us; Julia and everyone think we working," Mattie replied.

Estella smiled; she knew her mama would not be worried. "Well then, since y'all stayin' the night; I best be cookin' them greens I picked for supper, and Carl can kill a chicken for dinner," Ann told them.

"I can help and pick apples off that there tree in your back yard, and my Aunt Mattie could bake one of her great apple pies Estella told Ann."

Mattie and Estella went out the back door; on one side of the yard was a small chicken coop, where they found Carl plucking feathers from a chicken he had just killed. Nearby was a fire he made to boil the water he needed to pluck the feathers. Mattie and Estella stopped to talk to Carl for a minute. "I like the taste of chicken, but I hate the smell of hot wet feathers," Carl told them, still pulling feathers from the chicken that lay across a tree stump that had been painted on top with brown paint.

"I am glad you doin' that and not me," Estella said. Carl just smiled as they walked away. Seeing the four apple trees that lined the back of the yard, Estella pointed to the tree in the middle; saying, "That tree got some big apples!"

"Them apples way up too high, gal! And I ain't goin climb no tree today," Mattie said loudly.

"I've been climbing trees since I was knee high to a grasshopper! You just watch me."

Before Mattie knew it Estella ran toward the tree, grabbed a branch, and started climbing up the tree. Reaching the branches where the biggest apples hung, she called down to her Aunt, "I needs a bucket to put these here apples in."

Mattie found a pail that sat next to the side of the chicken coop and walked back to the tree. One by one Estella dropped the apples down to her Aunt. Before long, the pail was filled to the top with large red apples. Estella climbed back down the tree, saying, "I got the biggest ones; they goin' make a good pie." On the way back to the house they noticed Ann in the garden picking corn from plants that were nearly as tall as she was. They walked over to where she was picking the corn.

"Need some help?" Mattie asked.

"No—I only need to pull one or two more ears. "The three women walked back to the house discussing plans for supper.

"This bird is clean and ready for cooking," Carl said as he entered the house.

"We better get to cooking; it's goin' take a while to get the apple pie baked," Ann said as she dumped the pail of apples into a tub to be washed so they could be later placed in the pie. Estella helped Ann prepare for supper by cutting up the chicken, shucking the corn, and making potato salad while Mattie made and baked the apple pie.

Estella was hungry and looking forward to eating the feast on the table; but more than supper, she wanted to listen to the radio again. Over the next hour they all enjoyed the meal that everyone had worked to prepare.

"I know y'all want to hear the radio," Carl said, as he walked across the room to turn the dial on the radio, flooding the room with the sound of an orchestra playing "Moon Over Miami." Everyone continued to talk about the good meal. Estella, however, was lost in the beautiful music coming from the magic box on the other side of the room. When the music stopped a voice announced, "That was Eddy Duchin and the orchestra. What a great sound! Now here's our next selection from Guy Lombardo and his orchestra—'Red Sails in the Sunset.'" Estella leaned back in her chair, eyes closed, enjoying the music.

"Estella, why ain't you talkin'? You still listening to that there radio?" Mattie asked.

Before she could reply, Estella heard the announcer again. "I hope you liked our program; it has been brought to you by Lucky Strike. See you tomorrow; same time and same place on your radio dial."

"Y'all call it a radio, but I am goin' call it the magic box," Estella told Carl.

"That's a good name for it, Estella," Carl said.

As they finished the meal, the sound from the radio remained in the background, as Estella looked around the table at everyone. Everyone was laughing and talking. If she didn't know better she would think everyone had lots of money and the Depression was over.

The next morning, after breakfast, Mattie and Estella prepared to go back home. As their wagon headed down the road to Money, Mattie noticed Estella did not talk much. "What you thinking, gal?" Mattie asked.

"I just been thinking how much I miss Zac."

"Gal, you goin' be seeing that boy soon enough." Mattie looked at her and laughed. "You got a bad case of first love."

"I don't know if I love him, but I sho do like him a lot." Estella responded.

"We here!" Mattie said as she steered the small wagon into the front of Estella's shack.

The front door opened, with Julia and Leroy walking out. "Hi y'all doin'?" Julia called out as she moved toward the wagon. Estella jumped down and gave her mother a big hug. Mattie climbed down, giving Leroy and Julia a hug.

"How y'all like your new work, Mattie?"

"We think we goin' to be just fine. But we don't start 'til next week."

"Why's that, Mattie?" "It's a long story."

Just then, Paul came from the smokehouse carrying a small ham. Seeing Estella and Mattie he asked, "What y'all doin' back here so soon? I hope y'all ain't got fired already!"

"No we ain't been fired, Papa! We ain't even started yet!"

"Come on in the house and we'll tell you what happened," Mattie explained.

Leroy looked at Estella and rolled his eyes and said, "I bet y'all did get fired."

"You always don't know what you talkin' about, boy," Estella said as she pushed Leroy.

"Y'all stop that right now!" Julia called out.

"Now what's y'all story?" Paul asked. Mattie explained about how they would work three days a week and how big the house was where they would be working.

"We're goin' be making a dollar a day!" Estella interrupted, looking at Leroy with a big smile on her face.

"Well, now—that be a nice day's pay, mo' than the cotton fields," Paul told them. "And, befo' I forgets—that boy, Zac, stopped yesterday to say he would be back to see you. He wanted to know what day you was comin' home. I told him you would be back on Friday; he said he would come back then."

CHAPTER **24**

Leamon's Reply

Knowing that Zac was a man of his word, Estella prepared a picnic lunch of leftover food from Sunday's supper. As she packed napkins, spoons, and forks in the picnic basket her mother had made by hand, she heard a wagon outside the house. She washed her hands quickly and ran out the door to see Zac standing alongside the mule, tying him up to the tree near the house.

"Hi!" Estella shouted as she ran toward his waiting arms. The ground was still damp from the rain the night before, causing her to slip a bit. Zac leaned forward, catching her arm, and pulled her up next to him.

"I hope it ain't too wet for a picnic. I done fixed us a picnic basket full of food," she told him, smiling.

"I know a place that's nice and dry." He put his arms around Estella and pulled her closer to him. The air was hot and sticky; it had been raining a lot over the last few days. Estella moved closer to him; even the hot sun couldn't keep her away from him.

"I know a little place up the road where there's an old barn that done halfway fell on one side—but the other side look good," Zac told her as the wagon moved slowly down the tree-lined road. Every now and then the wind would blow, cooling them slightly.

Zac leaned over, saying, "I sho missed you, gal!" Estella looked up, feeling his welcoming lips. Her heart almost stopped, then started to beat fast. "Look up yonder—there's the place I was telling you about," Zac said, pointing to an old barn to their left. Zac steered the wagon onto a side road that ran in front of the barn. Estella noticed the river ran behind the barn.

"I like this place, Zac." Estella looked around her at the trees, the river, rabbits hopping around a nearby bush, and a blue jay flying overhead. Along the side of the barn were wild flowers in many colors: yellow, red, blue, and white covered the ground.

"I like it here too, gal, 'cause'n it's so quiet," Zac replied, holding her hand as they entered the barn.

The barn was just as Zac said it would be—one side had fallen to the ground, while the other side stood good and strong, as if someone or something had cut the barn down the middle.

"Why you think this barn only half good?" Estella asked.

"I think they put it up in two halves, not at the same time. The older part done fell down; the part where we standing been put up later." Zac pointed to a ladder that led to a loft. "Up there is a good place to have our picnic." She noticed that it was much cooler now that the roof was blocking the sun, and a strong wind blew through the barn because it was near the river.

Zac started up the ladder, with Estella behind him. When they reached the top, they found a nice dry floor covered with straw. At the rear of the barn, Estella could see the river flowing by. *This is a good place for a picnic,* she thought. Zac walked up behind her as she looked out at the river, wrapping his arms around her. She could feel his chest against her back.

"You one good-looking gal," he whispered in her ear.

Her heart started to beat like a tom-tom. She turned to face him. "You one good-looking guy, Zac," she whispered, staring up into his handsome face. For the next few minutes, Zac kissed her passionately, eventually kneeling down in the loft, pulling her toward him—his hands were gentle, yet eager to undress her. And before she knew it, Zac was on top of her, making her feel that deep desire to let him have his way with her.

After making love, the two lovers dressed and went for a walk down by the river. Holding hands, they walked down the riverbank. "What do you say we make it back to the barn and have that picnic we came here for?" Zac asked her.

Once back in the barn, they climbed the ladder to the loft. Estella opened the picnic basket that sat near the back of the loft. The sun started to go down a bit and it was much cooler, she thought, spreading a small blanket on the straw-covered floor. Zac took a piece of chicken from the basket and bit into it.

"Stop eating and help me," she told him.

"Well now, we got more food than five people could eat he said as he looked into the basket."

For the next few minutes, they ate and talked about home and Greenwood. "You know my Aunt Mattie done got me some new work up in Greenwood," Estella said.

"You goin' be moving to Greenwood?"

"No I ain't goin to move to Greenwood; I'll just be there three days a week."

"That's good," Zac said.

"I'm goin' be making a dollar a day. I think in a little while I'm goin' have enough money to go up North to Chicago."

Zac's face turned sad; his smile disappeared "When you goin do that?!" he said loudly. Estella was shocked at his tone.

"I don't know. I still got to save lots mo money, and it could take me a year fore I got enough." Zac face brightened a little. "Maybe you can go with me."

"I ain't planning on goin up North no time soon! I got things I have to do round these parts."

"We can talk about this later," she told him.

"I got something to deliver down the road from your place, so we best be gettin' started back." As he rose to his feet, Zac could only think about Estella going up North. As they rode back to her house, she could tell he was upset about her leaving. Arriving in front of her shack, Zac kissed and helped her down from the wagon.

"I ain't goin' in; like I told you, I got some shine to deliver." Before she could reply, his wagon started back down the road. She knew Zac was upset about her going North, but she also knew that going North was going to be the best decision, in spite of Zac's feelings. She turned toward the house and saw her mother in the garden, picking greens. Julia looked up from her work to find Estella standing beside her.

"How was your picnic?" "It was fun, Mama!"

Julia just smiled, saying, "A letter has done come for you." "Who is it from?"

"Go see—I left it on the table."

Estella almost ran into the house to find the letter. She saw a white envelope lying on the center of the table. She picked it up and knew immediately that it was from her Uncle Leamon, when she saw the postmark from Chicago, Illinois in one corner. She had written him some time ago about coming up North. She ripped open the envelope to find a letter.

Dear Niece

Sorry it took me so long to write you. I been busy picking up coal and junk don't laugh I am making money doin' this. You ask if I had room for you, if you come to Chicago I show do, my place ain't big but you can sleep on the couch in the front room. Chicago is a lot better than down South. I ain't seen not one white only sign, you can sit next to white folks on the bus up here. You can eat in the same place they eat; it took me a time to get use to all of this. The houses are bigger here, there are cars everywhere they got night clubs and movies. Write me and let me know when you are coming and I will meet you at the train or bus station. Tell everybody I said hello.

Love, Uncle Leamon

Estella ran out the house to show her mother the letter. Since her mother could not read very well, she read the letter to mother, who stood with her hands on her hips as she listened. As she finished reading, Estella looked up for her mother's reaction.

"Good to hear Leamon's doin' real good up North—that boy sho know how to make money anywhere he go. You sho want to go to Chicago bad," her mother said.

"I sho do, Mama! Things better up there." "You got money for your fare, gal?"

"Not yet—but I will in a little while."

"Well, you grown; so you can do what you want to do."

Leroy had come up behind them without them knowing it. "When you go up North, it's goin be good for me—cause I ain't goin' have nobody to boss me; Elizabeth too small."

Estella just rolled her head from side to side and placed her hands on her hips, saying, "You goin' miss me, boy, when I go up North."

"You two stop it right now." Their mother scolded them. They were interrupted by the sound of a wagon within a few feet of where they stood talking.

"Hi y'all doin'?" a voice called out— it was Mattie. "I just come by to make sho Estella ready for work in the morning."

"I goin' be good and ready for work when you get here, Auntie!" "You know she ain't talk 'bout nothing but your new work and making a dollar a day. Y'all goin be making that? A dollar a day?" Julia asked.

"That's what Pat told us," Mattie said with a big smile on her face.

"Who's Pat?" Julia asked.

"She's the maid to the Brolds. That's what she gets paid. Well, I got to be gettin' on—see y'all in the morning." With that, she turned walked back to her wagon and rode off. Estella knew she would have to save more than just her fare to Chicago. She had been saving every penny she got in a small tin box, which she hid at the base of a tree in a hole she dug and covered to match the ground nearby.

She was always careful not to let anyone see her when she was near her hiding place. She knew if anyone saw her, they could take the money from the tin. She quickly counted fifty-two dollars and twenty-five cents; that was what she had saved. It was a lot of money, but she wanted enough to live on for five or six months up North. *If she could save seventy or eighty dollars, that would be enough for the train ticket and pocket money,* she thought. Estella placed the tin back in the hole after she counted the money, carefully covering it.

"Estella—where you at? Supper ready; don't let it get cold!" her mother called from the house.

Estella ran back to the house, hoping she would make the rest of the money she needed at her new work in Greenwood.

CHAPTER **25**

A Sad Farewell

Early the next day, Mattie arrived. Walking into the kitchen, she said, "Gal, you ready? We don't want to be late our first day." "Shhhhhh, Auntie—everyone is still asleep." Estella placed a finger to her lips.

"Sorry!" Mattie said in a soft voice.

Estella grabbed a sweater from the hook next to the door and closed the door behind them lightly. They boarded the wagon outside and headed off for Greenwood as the sun rose in the sky.

"How long do you think Mrs. Brold will keep working us, Auntie?"

"I don't know, but it will be good for long as she do. You think you goin' to like the family?" Mattie asked Estella.

"To me they looked nice."

The sun was rising fast now, giving the sky and pink and blue color. "We're here," Mattie said as the wagon arrived in front of the Brold's big white house.

"Look like everybody sleep," Estella said, as they got down from the wagon.

"We don't want to wake them. Let's see if Pat is up—she sleeps in the coach house out back." They headed toward the small house in back of the garden. Before they could knock, the door opened and Pat came out.

"I am glad y'all didn't wake the family," she said.

"We know better!" Mattie said. They all laughed softly.

"Y'all come on in so we can talk," Pat said, as she walked into the house with Estella and Mattie behind her. "Y'all done ate?"

"No, but we ain't hungry," Estella replied.

"That's good, 'cause I eat after I fix breakfast for the family. We can all eat then. We eat and then clear the table and wash the dishes. Next I wash the clothes, and hang them out to dry. I dust and sweep up the house—I do half the rooms one day the other half next day. Since there's two of y'all, you can do the whole house in one day. And, one day a week I work the garden."

"What about the kids?" Mattie asked.

"They big enough to take care of themselves, and Mrs. Brold always see 'bout them. She used to have two maids but Lilly May got too old. She had been here since her mother come here, about the time slavery ended. Lilly May say this be the only place her mother know for work—and her too. And that dis family been good to her... paid her good, too. Her mother work for Mister Brold's daddy. Some folks say he the daddy of one of Lilly May's two kids. Y'all know how that got to be?" Estella and Mattie nodded.

"Negro women ain't got no rights in this here South," Mattie said.

"Maybe one day they goin' find out we people, just like everybody else," Estella explained.

"You right, but we best be gettin' to work. Y'all just follow me all day, and I'll show y'all what Mrs. Brold wants you to do."

Estella and Mattie followed Pat all day as she explained the work they would be doin'. They liked Pat; she was always smiling and looked happy.

"Mrs. Brold is a good person to work for. The rest of the family is okay, but you got to watch Peter. He's sixteen and always patting and feeling; you know how young white boys can be around Negro women," Pat said, rolling her eyes. The women talked about many things as they worked: the Depression, how Negroes were treated in the South, family, President Roosevelt's programs, gardening, and even radio programs.

"I think things are goin' to get better," Mattie said.

"When Auntie Mattie? I hope it's befo' I die," Estella replied.

Before long their first day of work was over; as they left the Brold house, Estella told Mattie she thought she would have the money to go North soon. "Why you think that?" Mattie asked.

"Cause this work pays good, Auntie!" "Do you got any money saved, girl?"

"I sho do, but I want to have lots mo befo' I go North." "When you think you goin' go North?"

"Maybe next year—it will take me that long to save the money I need." Estella was glad to reach the Jessup's house. Ann was fixing supper of fried catfish, corn on the cob, greens, and peach pie.

"I'm glad you don started fixin' supper; I am hungry, Ann," Mattie said.

"You need some help," Estella asked.

"No y'all—just sit down and enjoy supper." "I'll set the table," Estella told Ann.

They all sat down and ate until they had their fill. Estella rushed her food down because Carl always turned on the radio after supper. Today was no different; he rose from the table, walked over to the radio, turned the dial, and the room filled with the sound of The *Amazing Interplanetary Adventures of Flash Gordon*. Flash, Dale, and Dr. Zarkov were trying to get away from *Ming the Merciless*. Estella loved this show. She had seen it in the used newspapers her granddad sometimes brought home when white people threw them out. Mattie listened to the radio and liked the show almost as much as Estella did. Carl listened from his big red chair that Mr. Gray had given him. He asked, "Y'all think people goin' fly away to another planet like that Flash Gordon?"

"I think so; they already flying in them airplanes," Estella replied. "Well now; maybe people will get along better on another planet, 'cause they sho don't on this one! White peoples keep us Negroes down; rich ones keeps the po' folks down; one kind of church don't get along with the other kind of church. And some peoples tear down what others put up," Mattie said.

"Auntie Mattie, I think you trying to take Reverend Lockwood's place." They all laughed; even Ann, who had been in the kitchen, joined in.

"Say, Ann and Carl, I wondered is it still all right fo' me and Estella to stay with y'all while we work at the Brold house?"

"Sho 'nuf, Mattie. You know y'all like family to us. It be the smart thing to do, and save y'all from goin' back and forth to Money.

"That sho will be fun," Estella explained.

"I sho think I will like my new work," Mattie told Ann. "Staying here with y'all after work is goin' be nice."

The day, weeks, and months went by. Estella worked and stayed in Greenwood and saved money, and before she knew it, a whole year had gone by. She had saved almost enough to go up North to Chicago. As she walked out of her house into the back yard and down to the big oak tree where her money tin was hidden, she dug the tin out of the ground and opened its top. With a big smile on her face, she knew she had finally saved enough money to go up North. But she also knew she would be leaving everything she knew. She would be missing her family, her friends, her church…and Zac. She would miss him a lot.

When Mattie came by to pick her up for work at the Brolds', Estella told her she would not be going to work at the Brolds' anymore because she would be going up North. Mattie was shocked— she knew Estella always talked about going up North and was saving up for it, but she had not told her she would be going this soon. "Gal, why didn't you tell me this here before now?" Mattie said, looking at Estella with a funny look on her face.

"I ain't told nobody 'til now. You the first one I done told. I ain't even talked to Mama, Papa, or Leroy. I just made up my mind now," she told Mattie.

"I got to be gettin' on," Mattie said. "Don't want to be late for work."

Estella walked back into the house just as Julia entered the kitchen to start breakfast.

"Did you forget something?" She asked Estella with a puzzled look on her face.

"No," Estella replied.

"I ain't going to work today or no mo'."

"What you mean?" Julia said, with a puzzled look still on her face.

"You know that letter I got from Uncle Leamon a while ago?" "I reckon so," Julia responded.

"Well, he said in the letter if I come to Chicago on the sixth of this month he would meet me at the train station. I wrote him back and told him I had enough money for my fare and to live on for a while."

"Gal, the sixth is just two weeks away."

"I know—that's just enough time for me to pack up my things and say goodbye to everyone in Money."

Her mother put her hands on her hips, with a big smile. "You always were one strong-willed gal."

Leroy entered the kitchen, hearing only part of what was being said. "She strong and hard-headed, too!" Leroy said, laughing.

Estella pushed Leroy lightly. "I ain't goin' have to put up with you much longer."

Leroy had a puzzled look on his face. "What do you mean? What she mean, Mama?"

"Your sister says she's goin' up North to Chicago."

"You goin' to Chicago?" he asked, looking as if he had been hit over the head with a hammer.

"What goin' on in here?" her Grandfather called out as he entered the room.

"She say she goin' to Chicago, Paul."

Looking surprised and sad, he looked at his granddaughter and said, "When is this goin' happen? You got enough money for your fare?" Paul asked, as he walked toward the front room. He didn't wait for her to respond, pointing out the window, saying, "This here house in Money is small; Greenwood is a little bigger and the state of Mississippi is even bigger. Just look out this here window...what do you see? This road that can take you to the train and that train can take you to a new world way away from here."

Over the next week, the family didn't talk too much about Estella leaving Money; it was both happy and sad for her and her family. As she worked in the garden that afternoon, her mother said, "One week ain't a long time to get ready—to go so far from home."

Leroy and Paul came from the fields, as Estella noticed a tear roll down her mother's face.

"Why you crying, Mama?"

"'Cause I know you ain't goin be coming back to Money." Estella hugged her mother a long time, patting her on the back. "Let's get the rest of those tomatoes picked, 'fore it gets dark."

Estella felt sad about leaving her family, but knew her life would be better up North. The day passed by so quickly. Estella visited friends and family in Money and Greenwood. The visits were all the same, a mixture of sadness and happiness. Everyone was sad to see her go, but happy for her because they knew she would have a better life up North.

CHAPTER 26

Getting Ready

The sun rose bright in the sky on the day Estella had looked forward to for as long as she could remember. As usual, the July day was hot in Money; it was going to be a long time before she would be this hot again. The weather in Chicago was going to be cooler. Everything was going to be different for her in Chicago, she thought, as she closed the suitcases she had borrowed from her Aunt Mattie.

"Gal, you got all your packing done?" Julia yelled as she watched Estella put as much as she could into two suitcases. "I told you not to put too much in them suitcases, 'cause'n that goin' make them too heavy for you to carry."

"I need everything I am putting in them, Mama."

"We can send some of your stuff to you later," her Grandfather added.

"Okay—I can take some of this stuff out of the suitcases so they won't be so heavy."

"What you goin' eat on the train?" her mother asked. "I can buy something to eat on the train."

"Oh, now you got the money to buy food on the train?" her mother said, laughing. "Gal, you better help me make something for you to eat on your way up North. If you take your own food you can save your money. I hears that sometimes Negroes get poor service and leftovers to eat, and you know you got to sit in the Negroes' car when you get on the train. Let me make you some sandwiches—and I got time to fry you some chicken. Don't just stand there; let's get started."

"Yes, Mama!" Estella hugged her mother as they walked into the kitchen.

She fixed peanut butter and jelly sandwiches and ham sandwiches, and placed fruit and a small jar of water into the picnic basket her mother had made. Her mother fried the chicken; after it cooled, she wrapped the chicken and two pieces of cake in wax paper, putting everything in the basket.

"What time that train leave," Paul asked. "I think it leaves at five o'clock, Papa."

"You think, or does you know? Cause that train not goin' wait on you."

Estella took a piece of paper from her pocket. She had written the time on it when she stopped at the train station last week. She looked at the paper and told Paul it says the train leave at five o'clock today, and it got to Chicago at nine o'clock tomorrow morning.

"Well, it's three o'clock now and you ain't got but two hours befo' it pull out," Julia said.

"You better get a move on or you goin miss the train!" Leroy added, "You know I don't want you to do that!"

She knew her brother loved her as much as she loved him. They were going to miss each other—even his teasing. As she looked around at the only place she had ever lived—the yard, the trees, the

195

road, the mule and the old smoke house—she knew that each had been a part of her surrounding all of her life, and she would not see them for a long, long time…if ever again. She walked over to her bed and picked up her bags, walking into the front room where her family had gathered.

"I think I got everything, y'all."

"You better look around and make sure you ain't leaving nothin' you goin' need," Julia said.

"I got everything."

"I'll get your bags," Leroy said as he picked up the two suitcases and walked out to the wagon. Paul was feeding Joe the mule, who swished his tail at flies that buzzed around him.

"That gal ready yet?" Paul asked Leroy. "She says she is," Leroy replied.

"Well, tell her to get out here," Paul said. Julia was next to come out of the house.

"Y'all just don't stand there—get up on the wagon! We don't want that gal to miss her train."

The family loaded into the wagon—all but Leroy, who said he would walk. Estella knew this would be the last time she would go down this road, because now it was to the North.

Leroy walked alongside the slow-moving wagon. He called up to Estella, "I need to give this wagon a push so I can get rid of you faster." Then he let out a big laugh.

"I am goin' to be gettin' rid of you, too!" Estella yelled back.

Estella noticed as the wagon neared the train station that there were lots of people standing around. "Sho is a lot of folks at the station today."

"I know all these people!" Estella explained, as the wagon came to a stop in front of the station.

Estella looked about her—it looked like everyone she knew was there. The Jessups, Mattie, two Uncles she hadn't seen in a year or more, three cousins...even Mrs. Williams. But she didn't see Zac, and she wanted to tell him goodbye. Estella hugged and kissed everyone. Tears of joy and sadness rolled down everyone's face as they wished her well. A wagon pulled up and Zac jumped down, almost running toward Estella. "Sorry I am late." he said.

Zac was just about out of breath. He pulled Estella into his arms. The two of them forgot about all the others standing around them. "I am goin' miss you, gal."

"I am goin' miss you too," Estella said, with tears rolling down her face like rain falling from the sky. She knew she would miss Zac more than he knew. She would miss all the people here at the station today. Off in the distance, the sound of a steam locomotive grew louder and louder. Soon the big black locomotive came into view. Estella had seen this train and heard its whistle almost every day of her life—but today was different; it had come to take her away to a new life. Now the train was pulling into the station. The gray and black smoke coming from its stacks fanned out as it came to a stop. The sound of its bell rang out.

Steam puffed out above the wheels. The locomotive seemed to be alive as it hissed and puffed. Estella knew this was a ride she would never forget. A conductor jumped down from an open door of one of the coaches. He was dressed in a blue uniform. Four white people got off the train behind him.

"Watch your step!" he said, holding out his hand to help a well-dressed white lady down from the train. Estella saw two porters get off the train and walk into the station. They were dressed in white jackets and black pants. She had seen what many of the folks around

Money called "train people" all her life, because Money was located on a railroad line.

"Ten minutes, folks!" The conductor called out, as he walked down the platform.

Zac, still standing close to Estella, whispered in her ear, "You take care of yourself, gal—maybe someday I'll get up North."

"Hope you do!" she replied, through her tears.

Her mother came up to give her a big hug, with her Grandfather right behind her, saying, "Gal, you best remember the things I taught you, and you'll do just fine up North."

The two porters came out of the station talking, and the man who had taken her bags and put them on the train went by; the cart he was pushing was now empty. The train had four coaches painted dark green, with the words Illinois Center near the top over the windows. She saw the conductor take a watch from an upper pocket. Looking at it, he called out, "All aboard! The front two coaches are white only and the last two coaches are for Negroes only."

She knew that there were more Negro people than white people boarding; it was going to be crowded, she thought. The two porters stood next to the two open doors of the train, helping passengers onto the train. There were about fifteen people in the line ahead of her as she waited to board.

Julia and the rest of her family moved along beside her as the line got shorter. Estella soon saw that she would be next to board the train, so she turned to wave to her family and friends, tears rolling down from her eyes. Zac ran up to her and gave her one last kiss. The porter took hold of her arm. "Watch your step, miss," he said, as she took the first step into her new life—losing her balance and almost dropping her basket. Wiping the tears from her eyes, she stepped into the aisle, waiting for people ahead of her to put their bags in the overhead rack and sit down. The coach was almost full, but there were still a few seats empty at the back of the coach.

She placed her picnic basket and suitcase on the rack above, and quickly took one of the few empty seats by the window. Looking out, she could see her family and friends who stood on the platform outside, looking up at the train. She waved, and when they saw her they all smiled and waved back. Zac ran up toward the train waving and throwing kisses, while her brother Leroy made funny faces. She knew this scene of Zac and her family was one she would remember for a long, long time.

CHAPTER **27**

The Ride North

There were only four people to get on the train after Estella. They all seemed to be in one family: a man, a woman, and two children; each of them carried a bag and the woman was carrying a small basket almost like the one Estella had brought aboard. The four of them sat across the aisle from Estella in the last two empty seats besides the one next to her. Estella looked down the aisle and saw a short middle-aged woman coming toward her. Her hair was pulled back in a bun, with some gray hairs showing around her temples. She wore a flowered dress with a white collar, and her shoes looked like a pair her mother used to wear to church.

"Mind if I sit here?" she asked.

"You go right ahead," Estella said in a low voice. She watched her place two small boxes she was holding on the rack above them. "Hi. My name is Jane Jones—but most folks call me JJ." As she sat down on the seat beside her, Estella looked out the window one last time. She saw everyone was still on the platform waving, and she waved back. "All aboard!" she heard the conductor call out, and then she felt the train jerk forward—it was moving. Estella's heart was beating fast. Her mind was racing—she knew what she was leaving, but what was waiting for her up North she did not know.

"Well I am glad to be gettin' out of the South!" JJ said, as the train picked up speed.

"So am I", Estella replied."

For the next hour they talked about how long they had waited for this day and how hard life had been for them in the South.

"Where are you going, JJ?" "Memphis."

"Memphis ain't far enough for me; I want to get as far as I can from Mississippi, so I am going to Chicago. I got an Uncle there."

"Well, gal, you is lots younger than me—so Memphis be just fine for me!"

Estella looked out the window as the countryside rolled by. She had never been on a train before. She watched as farm houses, woods, lakes, roads, wagons, and fields flashed by her window. The train was moving fast now. Looking up she saw the conductor going from seat to seat saying, "Ticket please."

She reached into the pocket of her pants she was wearing and pulled out a yellow ticket with black lettering which read: Money, Mississippi to Chicago, Illinois—and on top of the ticket in big bold letters was Illinois Central Railroad, with the departure time and arrival time printed in the middle, and near the bottom it read, "Thanks for riding Illinois Central." Estella knew this was the piece of paper she had worked so hard for.

"Tickets, please." The conductor said, as he looked down at them. JJ handed him her ticket first, with Estella following.

"Thank you," he said, with a smile. Estella smiled back as the conductor took the tickets from the women across the aisle; turning away saying, "You folks enjoy the ride, now."

Estella watched the conductor as he walked back down the aisle and disappeared into the next coach. JJ said, "You know, that's the first time any white person smiled or told me to enjoy anything."

"First time for me, too—this going North is gettin' better already! "They both laughed. Estella noticed the family across the aisle fast asleep, except the woman.

"Look likes your family sleep," JJ said, looking across the aisle at the woman.

"I'm sorry I didn't tell y'all my name—it's May. And sleeping here by me is my two chi'len and my brother Willie. We're on our way to Memphis."

"I am goin' to Memphis too. I got family there," JJ said.

"So do we; maybe we can get to know each other better when we get to Memphis. I'll give you my Auntie's address in Memphis," May said, looking for something to write on. "You goin' to Memphis too?" May asked Estella.

"No, I am goin' to Chicago." "You got a long ride, gal."

"I know," Estella replied.

Estella saw the conductor coming down the aisle, calling out the next stop.

"Next stop Grenada—in ten minutes, folks." The conductor walked to the middle of the coach and then turned to enter the next coach. Estella looked up and saw three people standing up and taking things from the rack over their seats. The conductor re-entered the coach. "Out this way, folks," he said as he led the two women and a man to the doorway. Estella could tell the train had started to slow down as it pulled into Grenada. She looked out the window to see a small train station and a small town that, from what she could tell, was a little smaller than Greenwood. No one got on the train in Grenada; about ten minutes later the train continued down the tracks.

JJ and May continued to talk, being almost the same age, while Estella was much younger. She mostly listened as they talked about how things had been ten or fifteen years before she was born. May said her husband had stayed out in the field in the hot sun too long picking cotton and got a stroke and died four years ago.

The door at the front of the coach opened and a porter dressed in a white jacket entered the coach. He was carrying a tray filled with brown bags. "I got sandwiches here," he called out, holding up one of the brown bags. "Sandwiches just ten cents each—cold cuts, peanut butter and jelly, tuna, and ham. If you wish to buy one just raise your hand."

Estella saw five people raise their hands. The porter asked each of them what kind of sandwich they wanted. The porter walked toward where Estella was sitting and she recognized him—he was the same porter that had stopped in Money and left newspapers from time to time over the years.

The porter looked at Estella as he reached the area near her seat. "Don't I know you?" He asked. "You're Paul Reynolds' granddaughter?"

"I sho am," Estella said, glad to know someone on the train from her past.

"How is your Granddad?" "He's just fine."

"By the way, my name is Dan Wilson—what's your name?" "Estella."

"I think I remember your mama calling you sometimes when I stopped in Money. You were a young gal then. But I liked talkin' to your granddad—he is one smart man."

Estella smiled, hearing the porter talk about her Grandfather. "And where you ladies going?" The porter asked them.

"We both to Memphis," May answered.

"Looks like the rest of your family is sound asleep," the porter replied, smiling down at her sleeping children and brother.

"We had to walk five miles to this here train, and we had lots of stuff to carry, so I reckon they all tuckered out."

"Well, ladies, I got to get back to work."

"That porter sho is one good-looking man," JJ said as she watched him walk away. They all giggled.

The three women talked about life in Mississippi and the South. "Life in the South ain't all bad," Estella told them. "I had some good times in Money. I remember picnics, field days, hay rides, big family dinners, fishing—and most of all my friends and family."

"Y'all can say what y'all want bout how much fun and good times you had in Mississippi and down here in the South," May said looking at JJ and Estella with a frown on her face, with tears forming in her eyes. "My husband would still be here if 'n he didn't pick cotton in the hot sun in Mississippi."

"None of us would be on this train if Mississippi was a good place for Negroes to live," May added.

"I know the South would be better off if they stop mistreating Negroes and see we people just like white folks, only we got a different skin color," JJ said.

"I don't want y'all to think I like having to say yes ma'am and no ma'am, yes sir and no sir to people just 'cause they white, Negroes get shot, beat and hung—'cause some white people think they God." Estella wanted to make sure everyone know she didn't like Mississippi or the South.

A bald-headed man in the seat in front of Estella and JJ looked over the back of his seat, saying, "Amen, sister, to all you just said."

"Next stop, Pleasant Grove, in about ten minutes, folks," the conductor called out as he re-entered the coach. Estella looked up to see a man in bib overalls rise to his feet and walked to the front of the coach. The train slowed down and came to a stop at Pleasant Grove. "This here town ain't much bigger than Money. I ain't seen a big city yet," Estella said, looking over to JJ.

"Memphis is next. Now that's a big city! You will see one soon!" May said, looking across the aisle at Estella.

"Y'all want some of my fried chicken?" She asked. "Can you reach my basket, JJ?"

"Yes, is it the big brown one up here?" JJ asked, reaching up to retrieve the basket. She handed the basket to Estella. The smells of fried chicken, ham, and peanut butter came rushing out when she opened the basket.

"Now that chicken sho smell good!" JJ said as Estella handed her a piece and passed one across the aisle to May's waiting hand. The train began to slowly pick up speed as they pulled away from the town of Pleasant Grove.

"This here chicken is real good," May said, as she bit into the drumstick. "You sho know how to cook chicken."

"I didn't cook it—my mama did, and people say she cooks the best chicken in Money."

"I hope my folks don't wake up fo' I eat my chicken," May said, looking over at her sleeping family.

"Look!" Estella said, pointing toward the window. "What lake is that?"

"Girl—that ain't no lake; that is the Mississippi River," JJ told her. Estella didn't reply. This was the first time she had seen the Mississippi River. All her life she had heard about the Mississippi River; now she knew why folks talked about the mighty Mississippi.

"The river is where Mississippi got its name," JJ said.

"I've been on this train before," May said, "and the river gets real big when you get to Memphis."

The train was racing toward Memphis at a high speed, as it crossed country road after country road. Estella could see the black smoke billowing into the air, passing her window; as she looked out at the countryside it became a blur as the train went faster and faster. The three women talked about the Depression and when things would get better. Before they knew it, the conductor was calling out:

"Memphis in about twenty minutes, folks."

"We in Memphis already? Look how big the river done got!" Estella was like a child in a candy store, looking out the window.

May shook her brother and children, waking them. "Y'all better wake up befo' we miss our stop."

Willie rubbed his eyes and shook the boy next to him. "You got to wake up, boy. We done slept all the way to Memphis," Willie explained.

Once more Estella felt the train slowing down as it neared Memphis. The houses got closer and closer as Memphis grew near and nearer. She pressed her face to the window, anxious to see Memphis come into view. "Look at that!" she said, seeing downtown Memphis. "I ain't never seen no buildings that tall."

JJ laughed at the young girl, as she and May stood up, collecting their bags to leave the train.

Estella noticed May and her family was already standing in the aisle. Glancing down at Estella, May said, "I hope you have a good ride up to Chicago."

"Thank you! It was nice to meet you, your family—and you too JJ," Estella told her.

JJ gave Estella a quick hug, and off they all went down the aisle toward the front of the coach. The conductor walked up the aisle, announcing, "This way, folks," as about fifteen people followed him.

CHAPTER 28

A Whole New World

The train came to a stop at the station that sat between the downtown and the Mississippi River. Estella watched as the coach emptied out, about half its passengers leaving. Looking out the window, she saw people on the platform, Negro and white, as they met and embraced people who had been waiting for them. She was surprised at the size of Memphis and how many cars, wagons and trucks she saw—more than she had ever seen in one place. She watched as new passengers entered the coach; the passengers getting on the train seemed to be better dressed than the ones who had just gotten off the train.

She saw a large woman coming toward her. "Can I sit here?" the woman asked, pointing at the seat JJ had just left.

"Yes, it's fine with me, ma'am." She noticed the woman was not carrying bags.

"Hi—my name is Hattie," the woman said, as she sat down next to her. "What's your name?

"Estella—that's a pretty name."

There had been lots of room when JJ sat next to her but Hattie filled her seat and threatened to spill onto Estella's seat.

"Where you going?" Hattie asked, with a big smile. Her round face always seemed to be smiling.

"Chicago," Estella replied.

"You got a ways to go, gal! Me, I am just goin a hop, skip and jump up to Fulton. You know where that is?"

"No, ma'am; where is that?"

"It's in Kentucky; you ever been to there?"

"No, I ain't never been out of Mississippi 'til now." *Hattie sure asked a lot of questions*, Estella thought. "I got to get up and get a drink of water." She had been sitting since she got on the train. "I need to move my legs a little," Estella said.

Hattie rose to her feet to let Estella get into the aisle. As she walked down the aisle, Estella noticed every seat was full; some people had babies and children with them. She heard people talking as she continued to walk. Suddenly, the door to the coach opened and the porter entered, coming toward Estella. "I was just coming to see you," he said. She was surprised at his words. "You hungry, Estella?"

"Yes, a little."

"That's good, 'cause me and Mike, the other porter on this train, got room for you at our little table behind the kitchen. I asked the conductor and he said it was all right long as we got our work done."

She didn't know what to think. "Okay…you mean now?"

"No. Go back to your seat and I'll come and get you later." Estella placed a small paper cup under the fountain, filling it with water. She drank the water down fast, and then drank a second cup before returning to her seat.

When she returned to her seat, she found Hattie had moved into her seat next to the window and was fast asleep. So she sat down next to the sleeping woman.

"All aboard!" the conductor called out a little while later; she felt a bump, and the train was moving again. Suddenly, a loud noise came from the sleeping woman next to her. She was familiar with the noise—her Grandfather snored in his sleep too. *This ain't goin' be no fun*, she thought to herself. As the train picked up speed twenty minutes later, she saw the porter coming minutes later, she saw the porter coming "Are you ready for some good hot food?" He asked.

"I sho am," she said, glad to have the porter rescue her from the snoring woman. She followed him through the coach into the whites-only coach. She could feel eyes on her, but since she was with the porter, she knew it would be all right. They entered the next coach, where white people sat eating and talking. The train kitchen was behind a wall at the end of the dining coach they had just walked through; the smell of food filled the air in the kitchen. The porter led her to a small booth at the back of the kitchen.

"This is where us porters and train workers eat," he said, smiling, and pointed at the booth. "Have a seat." She took a seat in the booth next to the window. She felt the train speed down the track and heard its steam whistle blowing for a crossing. "Now you just sit right there—I'll be right back with a plate in a jiffy."

She looked around, seeing a small room off to her right and a washroom next to it. The door at the front of the coach had a sign that read "EMPLOYEES ONLY". She could still see the conductor through a window in the door. She watched as he took two plates from above the stove that sat in the middle of the kitchen; then he walked back to the booth where Estella was sitting.

"I got our plates ready," he explained, placing two plates on the table in front of her. She looked down to see a salad, a baked potato, and the biggest steak she'd ever seen. "Oh, by the way—we are serving a great dinner wine tonight," he said with a smile and a wink. "I got about forty-five minute befo' we get to Fulton," he said, as he took a seat across from her. "Don't let your food get cold."

She started eating, thinking how great this day had been so far—everything was so new. She had left home, boarded a train, met new people, seen a big city for the first time, and had seen how big the Mississippi river was—now she was sitting here having a porter on the train serve her this great meal. She had seen so much since leaving Money.

"This here salad taste so good," she said, biting into a tomato. "Don't let that potato get cold." The porter asked, "How's your family doin' down in Money?"

"Good. I mean ain't nobody sick. Thank you, Mr. Porter, for all this food and being so nice to me."

"You don't need to say Mr. Porter; remember my name is Dan. It's okay for you to call me Dan…it sounds better than Mr. Porter." They both laughed. "I watched you grow up. The good thing about being porter is you get to see the whole country, meet all kinds of people…everyday people to big shots."

She wanted to know more about what Dan did, and what he had seen.

"I want you to tell me 'bout what you do as a porter, Dan." "Well, I am part of a train crew I help passengers on and off the train. The porters help with baggage, and we help the cook and kitchen staff. Some of the places I have been are from Chicago to Los Angeles, from Chicago to New York, and this run from Chicago to New

Orleans. Some of the people I have met include Joe Louis, Babe Ruth, Cab Calloway, Amelia Earhart, Jack Benny, Fats Waller, and Louis Armstrong…too many for me to recall. I sometimes see bad weather. One time we had to stop because of all the dust in Nebraska, and sometimes we see tornados off in the distance. And on these here trains, I see rivers, hills, forests, farms, swamps, mountains, towns, and cities; the more I see, the more there is to be seen. This is one big wonderful country."

What Dan said was amazing to her. All this time, living in the South, she had thought it was just the South that was bad. Now it looked like she was right. Dan went on to say how he saw that Negroes were leaving the South by the trainloads.

"Every time I do a run coming from the South to the North, the train is full of Negroes coming North like you. The trains goin' South ain't got half the Negroes as the ones goin' North.

"I ain't never seen no Negro man say how good and wonderful this country is!" she told him.

"That's 'cause you been in the South all your life."

"In Money all we did is work in the fields from sun-up to sun-down. We goes to a small bad school with bad books—the teachers did the best they could with what they had. We got to always bow down to white folks. And we always so poor."

"I know," Dan said, looking around to see if anyone else was nearby to hear him. "In my work, I see more than most Negroes will ever see. That's why I and other porters drop off the newspapers in places like Money, so Negroes will know things are better up North. In Chicago you don't have to bow down to nobody. Now don't get me wrong—the North is far from perfect, but it's a lot better than the South for Negroes."

She noticed it was dark outside; she could see only a few lights off in the distance.

"I got to get back to work," Dan said. "You can sit here as long as you like to finish up your meal." Dan got up from the booth, saying, "I like helping and talkin' to young Negroes from the South. I like letting them know this is a great country that need to fix a few things."

Dan walked back through the kitchen into the dining coach. Estella finished her food, then walked back through the train to her seat. She got funny looks from white people as she passed by and the same looks from Negroes as she passed them in the coach to find her seat. She arrived at her seat to find Hattie still asleep, and she was snoring even louder now. But she was now full of good food and sleepy. She took her seat, and it wasn't long before she too was fast asleep.

"Fulton, next stop!" The conductor called out. Both Estella and Hattie jumped, being awakened from a deep sleep.

"That's my stop!" Hattie said, looking up at the conductor. "We'll be stopping in Fulton in about ten minutes, folks."

"I got to get ready to get off," Hattie said, looking over at Estella. "Let me get out of your way." Estella moved into the aisle so Hattie could move past her.

"It's been nice meeting you," Hattie said, as she moved into the aisle. The two women stood talking for a few moments, feeling the train slow down.

"This way out," the conductor announced, as he came into the coach. Hattie followed the conductor down the aisle, and then disappeared. Two other people also get off the train at Fulton. No one got on the train. She was glad no one got on the train, because now she would have two seats all to herself. She returned to her seat next to the window, and fell asleep. A short time later, Estella woke up to the shock of her life. At first she thought she was dreaming that a white woman was sitting in the seat next to her. In all her life, no white person had ever sat next to her. Fear washed over her…had this woman made a mistake of some kind?

"Hi, my name is Sophie. What's your name?"

"My name is Estella, but you better go see the conductor, 'cause you sitting in the wrong place," Estella said softly.

"But the conductor is the one who told me to sit here."

She couldn't believe her ears. She looked down the aisle to see that other white people were sitting next to Negroes.

"Why did you say I was in the wrong place?"

"In da South, white folks and Negroes ain't supposed to sit together." She noticed the woman's voice sounded different.

"Well now, don't you worry, I know the world is a funny place; people always doin' bad things to other people. In my country, Germany, a Nazi raped and shot my mother. My father and I had to get out of Germany because Jews were being beaten. Their businesses were being taken from them too. My father sold his business and got us out of Germany right after the Nazi killed my mother. I always ask myself why things are the way they are."

Estella was speechless, as Sophie told her about things in a country called Germany. This was the first time she had ever heard about white people being so mean to other white people.

"I guess I am doin' all the talkin'," Sophie added, as she took an apple from a bag in her lap. "Tell me about your country."

"My country?" Estella mumbled. "Yes, your country," Sophie replied.

"I never thought about America being my country. In this country the white folks be in control of everything…it is not good to me or any other Negro. In this country the land is beautiful, but for people like me—Negroes—we just get to do lots of work for almost no pay, we go to school that ain't as good or big as the white folks' school, we always get to make whites think they better than us. If a white person tells you to do something, you just say yes ma'am, yes sir… even if they are the same age as you. They treat us like you say them people treat your people in Germany."

Sophie just sat and listened to her talk about all the things she had lived through in the South—the shootings, the lynchings, and the hard work in the cotton fields.

"I don't know much 'bout the rest of the country, but I sho hope it ain't like Mississippi," Estella explained. Sophie realized the two girls had a lot in common—the terrible things people did to each other.

"What's a Nazi?" Estella asked.

"A Nazi is a person who believes in the Nazi party, which is not like the Democratic or Republican party in this country, where we believe in the Constitution and the Bill of Rights. A man named Adolph Hitler, who is a very bad man, runs the Nazi party."

"The Nazi party sounds like the Ku Klux Klan to me, 'cause they treat Jew people like the Klan treat Negroes in the South." Estella explained. "One time I saw a movie and it was talking bout that Hitler man when my boyfriend Zac took me to the movies. I never thought I would know people from over there."

Just then they noticed Dan standing in the aisle next to their seat. Sophie got up to get a drink of water at the front of the coach, asking him to excuse her as she moved past him in the aisle.

"Dan, how come white folks can sit next to Negroes now; but not in Mississippi?"

In a low voice Dan replied, "Shhhh, we in the North now, when we crossed the Ohio River, we ain't in the South no mo'. It don't make sense to me why you can sit next to white people on one side of the river and not on the other, I think sometimes this country is two countries in one. Well, Estella, I needs to go—we gonna be in Chicago soon."

Estella watched as he moved down the aisle, passing Sophie coming back up the aisle to her seat. She and Sophie talked for a while, until the conductor came up the aisle, saying, "Chicago in about twenty minutes. Chicago will be our last stop."

Looking out the window, Estella could see the road that ran next to the train tracks, seeing more cars than she had ever seen before. She also noticed that the farm fields had given way to houses that grew closer and closer together. The houses gave way to small buildings, then tall buildings. She also noticed a light fog was starting to form.

Sophie looked out the window and said, "I think it's gettin' foggy."

Estella was getting very excited; she saw that people had started to get their bags and packages down from the overhead rack. Estella knew that when she stepped off this train, her life would never be the same. Her heart started to beat fast as she stood up to get her belongings from the rack above her seat.

"Chicago in ten minutes!" the conductor called out.

Sophie was now standing in the aisle as the train slowed. "I hope your move to Chicago will go well."

Everyone was standing in the aisle, waiting for the train to come to a stop.

"This way out, folks!" the conductor called out.

Slowly the people in the aisle moved forward, and at last Estella reached the door of the train, which was now inching toward the platform. She had worked so hard for this moment; now she was in the North and in Chicago.

The conductor took her by the arm as she stepped off the train, saying, "Watch your step miss," he said.

Estella stepped carefully down each step—she was just a few steps from her first time being in the North—she was almost shaking—she could hardly believe it. As the fog rolled in from Lake Michigan, it surrounded her and the other passengers. Fear now took over, because she could not see more than two feet in front of her, and she couldn't see anything—let alone her Uncle Leamon. She thought—*What if he is not here?* She had his address on a piece of paper, but she knew the address—she had read the paper a hundred times—1011 S. Canal Street. She tried to see through the passengers ahead of her, who seemed to be disappearing into the mist…just a few feet ahead of her.

Where was Uncle Leamon? She saw a Negro man who looked like Leamon, but as he came out of the fog, to Estella's disappointment, it was not her Uncle. The fog made it hard to see anything or anyone clearly. Estella looked into the fog as if her eyes could see through it, and suddenly the figure of a man stepped out of the mist.

Estella cried out, "Uncle!"

She had never been so glad to see him. She hugged him so hard; he felt her tremble.

"How was your trip?" he asked. But she could not answer; tears ran down her face like a river. She stood there in front of her Uncle, crying, because had been long and hard.

TO BE CONTINUED...

CPSIA information can be obtained
at www.ICGtesting.com
Printed in the USA
JSHW012349120623
43075JS00002B/48